The Virginia
BLUE RIDGE
RAILROAD

MARY E. LYONS

The Virginia BLUE RIDGE RAILROAD

THE
History
PRESS

Published by The History Press
Charleston, SC
www.historypress.net

Copyright © 2015 by Mary E. Lyons
All rights reserved

First published 2015

Manufactured in the United States

ISBN 978.1.46711.893.4

Library of Congress Control Number: 2015947036

To my friend Margaret Ryther

Contents

Contents

A Note on Sources

My research for *The Virginia Blue Ridge Railroad* began at the Library of Virginia, which describes its records of the Board of Public Works as "rich in the details of the development of Virginia's internal improvements during the nineteenth century. Few collections in other archival institutions are comparable." Indeed, these papers are the principal source of information about the Blue Ridge Railroad and the Blue Ridge Tunnel, a nineteenth-century engineering marvel that is gaining its rightful place as a structure of national significance. The longest mountain railroad tunnel in the world upon completion, it was declared a National Historic Civil Engineering Landmark in 1976. This premier recognition of engineering achievement includes the Statue of Liberty, Washington Monument, Panama Canal and Eiffel Tower.[1]

No letters or journals written by the Irish famine immigrants and slaves who built the Blue Ridge Tunnel or other sections of the Blue Ridge Railroad have been located. Voluminous papers at the Library of Virginia are a helpful—if cold-eyed—substitute, but they are of minimal use without context. This history of the Blue Ridge Railroad offers a historical perspective for Board of Public Works papers pertinent to the laborers and the structures they built.

Additional documents consulted include the *Spectator* and *Vindicator* newspapers in Staunton, Virginia, and other newspapers around the state. Non-text sources—the most fascinating aspect of my research—include gravestone inscriptions, abandoned railroad track beds and stone culverts.

A Note on Sources

Silent survivors of the Blue Ridge Railroad, they are as essential as texts to understanding the lives of the laborers.

Since November 2009, I have assembled data from fifty sets of public records; typed ten thousand names and jobs listed on Blue Ridge Tunnel payrolls; compiled more than two thousand names from Brooksville Tunnel payrolls; and transcribed ledgers, diaries and slave lists. All were invaluable while writing this book, as a full history of the Blue Ridge Railroad cannot be told without them.

Preface

The Virginia Blue Ridge Railroad is a behind-the-curtain look at challenges that engineers, contractors and laborers faced in the state's push to reach the Ohio River by rail. Concurrently, it traces the arc of labor shortages and labor unrest during the 1850–60 construction decade. These two factors contributed as much to slow progress along the line as the hard greenstone that the men battled daily with hand drills and gunpowder blasts.

Questions about labor on the Virginia Blue Ridge Railroad intrigued me from the moment I learned that Irish immigrants and hired slaves built it. I wondered if they worked shoulder to shoulder and if conflict occurred, as happened on canal and railroad construction in Maryland in the 1830s. How many men labored on the Blue Ridge Railroad? What were their wages, jobs and names? How did they come to work on the railroad, and were their lives typical of laborers on other antebellum railroad construction projects?[2]

My exploration of primary documents resolved all questions but the last. That answer proved elusive until I read David Gleeson's *The Irish in the South, 1815–1877*. Historians have long studied nineteenth-century Irish immigrants, but most of their publications focus on Irish living outside the South. Raw numbers may justify the emphasis. Of the 1.2 million Irish immigrants in America in 1860, only 10 percent settled below the Mason-Dixon line. Yet, as Gleeson points out, a look at how outsiders such as free blacks and Irish immigrants fared in the South can reveal much about antebellum society.[3]

As I read *The Irish in the South*, I was struck by how closely the experiences of Irish laborers on the Blue Ridge Railroad project—located in a rural area—matched those of other Irish immigrants in the region, including city dwellers. Among many other similarities, they were susceptible to disease, had a sharp business sense and were persecuted or marginalized for their Catholic religion. The lives of Irish immigrants along the tri-county Blue Ridge Railroad mirror those of other Irish in the antebellum South, with a notable difference. David Gleeson gives examples of conflict between Irish and black workers in Charleston, South Carolina; Natchez, Mississippi; and New Orleans, Louisiana. If comparable violence developed on the Blue Ridge Railroad during the construction decade, the news never reached the chief engineer, Claudius Crozet.[4]

Labor was uppermost in Crozet's mind because it was often scarce, and the Irish struck or threatened a walkout on average once a year. Had he known of struggles between the Irish and enslaved crews, he would have shared the information in his frequent, highly detailed letters to members of the Board of Public Works. Further, local and regional newspapers scrutinized every aspect of the state-funded Blue Ridge Railroad. They would have eagerly reported news of open conflict between the Irish and slaves.

Private clashes could have occurred, of course. In 1854, both Irish and slaves labored in the Blue Ridge Tunnel as floorers, clearing rocky debris in wheeled carts that ran along work rails. Claudius Crozet apparently kept the two races apart, but there is only one way out of an un-bored tunnel. An Irish floorer, angered by Crozet's manipulation of Irish wages with slave labor in late 1854, easily could have tossed an insult toward a slave or struck a blow while passing him in the dark, deafeningly noisy passage. Beyond this scenario or the possibility that a yet-unseen primary document with proof might surface, there is no evidence of conflict between Irish and slave laborers on the Blue Ridge Railroad.[5]

Racial harmony on railroad construction in Virginia was not unheard of in the 1850s. Black and Irish railroad workers toiled side by side in Prince Edward County for the Southside Railroad in 1854 and visited one another's shanties at night—possibly to end the working day with a shared pull of whiskey, as did Irish and black laborers at urban saloons in the antebellum South. The Southside and Blue Ridge Railroad examples may be anomalies. Or, they may be consistencies that invite a more nuanced interpretation of labor disturbances in southern states.[6]

The presence of slaves did not cause labor unrest on the Blue Ridge Railroad. Rather, Irish discontent was directly related to wages and working conditions, and the spilling of Irish blood in violent construction accidents almost always presaged demands for higher pay. Claudius Crozet's letters to the Board of Public Works show that he was an unreliable correspondent regarding the numerous Irish injuries and deaths on the railroad. Save for the 1854 cholera epidemic, he seldom mentioned them and then only in the context of a work slowdown. Perhaps he was being politic, putting the best face possible on what was often disappointing news about the railroad construction. Or he and the board may have considered Irish laborers dispensable, as was often the case on public works, and of little significance.

Whatever the reason, Crozet ignored the connection between fatalities and subsequent strikes in his letters to the board and in practice. For the Irish, though, strikes were a reasonable reaction to seeing the bodies of fellow workers blown up in blasts or skulls crushed by falling rock. Understandably, the men wanted fair compensation for waking up each morning to the knowledge that they might not survive the day.

East portal of the Blue Ridge Tunnel. *Author's collection.*

Acknowledgements

It takes a mighty crew to build a railroad book. The following individuals contributed encouragement, stories, contacts, research, images, advice or invaluable comments on drafts of the manuscript: Dale Brumfield, Ed Cohen, Art Collier, Paul Collinge, Michael Dixon, Tom Dixon, Mary Lee Dunn, Marilyn Edwards, Allen Hale, Jane Harrington, Blacksnake Jim Kauffman, Ron Michener, Ciarán Reilly, Margaret Ryther, Jane Smith, Lucia Staunton, Sam Towler, Judy Underwood, archivist Karen Vest at the Waynesboro Public Library and J.C. Watson. I also owe deep thanks to the Virginia Foundation for the Humanities for an affiliate fellowship that has made my ongoing research possible.

BIRTH OF A RAILROAD

The Virginia Blue Ridge Railroad, built between 1850 and 1860, never sold a ticket or hired a stationmaster. The tracks, which passed through three central Virginia counties, were only 16.81 miles long. Yet this short distance was an essential link in a much larger public works project that encompassed two impenetrable mountain chains, construction by three railroad companies and 423 miles of track through ten counties—five in Virginia and five in what is now West Virginia.[7]

A train journey on Amtrak's Cardinal from Charlottesville through the Blue Ridge and Allegheny Mountains to Huntington, West Virginia, gives an idea of the geographical scale of the entire venture, as does the same trip by automobile on Interstate Highway 64. Both scenic excursions are a matter of hours and taken for granted now. Before the coming of the Blue Ridge Railroad, the journey meant slow, aching days of stagecoach, wagon or canal travel around the mountains or across mountain passes. Finding a faster route through the two ranges was imperative. It would end the isolation of citizens west of the mountains who, living far from the capital city of Richmond, felt they had little power in running the state. A quicker way through the Blue Ridge would also greatly expand trade between the Tidewater region and the fertile Shenandoah Valley.

Portly Claudius Crozet was the first to envision the possibility of this impossible route. Born in France in 1789, he studied mathematics and science at the École Polytechnique. He then became an artillery officer in the army of Napoleon I. During Napoleon's invasion of Russia, Crozet was held prisoner at

View of the Blue Ridge Mountains from Rockfish Gap, Virginia. *Author's collection.*

the home of a Russian nobleman who treated him as an esteemed guest. After Crozet's release, he returned to Paris and married Agathe DeCamp.[8]

Napoleon's exile to the island of Saint Helena marked the end of the first phase of twenty-six-year-old Crozet's life. It was time to try his fortunes across the sea, where plans for inland transportation projects such as the Erie Canal were underway. With a recommendation letter from the Marquis de Lafayette in hand, and an imperfect knowledge of the English language, Crozet immigrated with his wife to the United States in 1816. The United States Military Academy at West Point hired him as assistant professor of engineering that same year.[9]

The engineer's talents were soon apparent to the State of Virginia, which had recently formed its first Board of Public Works. The state

Mid- to late nineteenth-century railroad bond. Images of trains, surveyors, laborers and tools symbolize the industrial age. *Author's collection.*

needed someone of Crozet's caliber to conduct land surveys, create maps and advise it on transportation routes. Crozet fulfilled all these duties as Virginia's chief engineer from 1823 to 1831, 1837 to 1843 and 1849 to 1857. His contemporaries described him as "irritable, intolerant of anyone who disagreed with him, and unpopular." But the fractious Frenchman saw what others in Virginia could not initially see, and he saw it on horseback, probably accompanied by a slave who carried his surveying tools.[10]

Crozet and engineers under his supervision thoroughly toured the state in the 1820s and 1830s, weighing the practicalities of turnpikes, railroads and canals. He concluded in 1831 that a "railroad is undoubtedly the system I should prefer…if Virginia is prepared to expend three millions of dollars upon an improvement up to the mountains, it is certainly not to a canal I wish to see them applied."[11]

Siphoning state and private monies from canal construction was politically unpopular with influential members of the general assembly who had invested in the waterways. The Board of Public Works lowered Crozet's salary in 1831, which forced him to resign, and then abolished the position of chief engineer. But it reinstated it two years later, and in 1837, as six new railroad companies in the state began laying tracks, the board again felt the need for Crozet's guidance. When it invited him to resume his job, he accepted.[12]

The chief engineer and his assistants then scoured the Blue Ridge Mountains, looking for a westward railroad route. "Our surveys have

View of Rockfish Gap from the east, 2014. *Author's collection.*

indicated that the most favorable pass is at Rockfish Gap," he wrote to the board in 1839. Recommending a tunnel about one mile long through the narrow cleft in the mountains, he predicted that railroads would "benefit the state by retaining and increasing its western population, clearing and settling an extensive territory, and adding to the revenue by the enhanced value of the lands traversed by them."[13]

After an economic depression led to state budget cuts in 1842, the Board of Public Works once again terminated the position of chief engineer. Crozet spent the next few years helping establish the Virginia Military Institute. Meanwhile, the urge for the added revenue he had forecast in 1837 eventually proved irresistible.[14]

On October 3, 1846, as summer's heat faded, a group of Augusta County dignitaries assembled at the courthouse in Staunton, Virginia—a city of hills that lies about fifteen miles west of Rockfish Gap. Calling themselves the Friends of Internal Improvements, they resolved, "Should the great lines of communication between the east and the west be completed, they [Augusta residents] feel assured that there will be…consequent increase in her wealth and population."[15]

During the next two years, seventeen Virginia counties and the city of Richmond joined Augusta's "Westward Ho!" choir. In early October 1848, their delegates convened in Staunton. They agreed that the general assembly should build a railroad toward the west, "having in view the ultimate extension to the most suitable point on the Ohio River."[16]

The delegates well understood the significance of the Ohio River, then the western border of Virginia. The confluence of the Ohio and Mississippi Rivers was the nation's greatest intersection, linking east with west and north with south. Eastern seaboard states could make fortunes by transporting goods and passengers to and from the watery highways. Virginia was not alone in its determined westward reach. From New York to Georgia, railroad companies along the eastern seaboard were punching through the Appalachians in the 1840s and 1850s as quickly as they could find immigrants and hired slave labor to blast the tunnels. One of six national contenders in the race for the Ohio River, Virginia's project was the most difficult because of rough terrain at Rockfish Gap. Crozet told the Board of Public Works that he "never saw any section of the same extent more complicated and rugged." He later referred to the eight miles east of the Blue Ridge Tunnel as "dangerous ground."[17]

In 1849, the privately owned Louisa Railroad operated between Richmond and Gordonsville and was laying tracks to Charlottesville. That year, it made preliminary plans to reach the Ohio River, adopting a new name that signified its route through the midline of the state: the Virginia Central. Subscriptions from citizens in counties along the planned line would finance the project, but the company lacked resources for the costly challenge at Rockfish Gap. The State of Virginia formed its own company, the Blue Ridge Railroad, to bankroll the seventeen difficult miles.[18]

From then on, the Virginia Central and Blue Ridge Railroads were intricately bound together in a private-public partnership. Construction took place simultaneously in Albemarle, Nelson and Augusta Counties as the two companies worked in tandem—sometimes sharing labor and materials, other times squabbling over them.

Bookending the east side of the Blue Ridge Railroad in Albemarle County, the Virginia Central agreed it would continue its rails from Charlottesville to Woodville (now Ivy) and then to Mechum's River. Blair Park plantation lay eight miles west of Mechum's. The Blue Ridge Railroad portion would begin at Blair Park, pierce the mountain at Rockfish Gap and wind down three miles to Waynesboro in Augusta County. Bookending the west side of the Blue Ridge Railroad, the Virginia Central would lay rails from

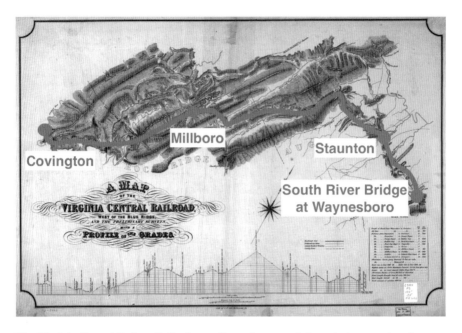

The Virginia Central Railroad's Covington Extension passed through the counties of Augusta, Bath and Alleghany. *Courtesy of the Library of Congress.*

Waynesboro to Staunton. At this stage of the planning, the Virginia Central was uncommitted to building the Covington extension. This part of the line would stretch west from Staunton through Bath County and on to Covington in Alleghany County.

A third state-funded railroad—the nascent Covington and Ohio—would approach from the west side of the state. It would begin at Big Sandy River, a tributary of the Ohio River; pass through White Sulphur Springs in Greenbrier County; and link with the Alleghany County tracks. When completed, the two sides of the state would finally touch hands.

As plans for the elaborate rail system took shape, two short but indispensable gaps remained. The Board of Public Works was undecided about which company—the Virginia Central or Blue Ridge Railroad—would lay tracks from Mechum's River to Blair Park in Albemarle County. The board was also unsure about which would build the Mechum's River Bridge in Albemarle and the South River Bridge in Augusta. These uncertainties plagued Claudius Crozet for the next three years.

Plans for the Blue Ridge Railroad tunnels, however, were firm. Most Blue Ridge Tunnel devotees know that the passage is almost one mile long and located seven hundred feet under the mountain at Rockfish Gap. Many are

The Blue Ridge Railroad tunnels. Original map corrected. *Courtesy of the Library of Congress.*

unaware, though, that the tunnel, albeit the onyx in the crown, was one of four built for the Blue Ridge Railroad. East to west, the three sister passages were the Greenwood, Brooksville and Little Rock Tunnels in Albemarle County. Little Rock Tunnel is still in use. Greenwood Tunnel closed when the Chesapeake and Ohio Railway blasted a parallel cut a few yards south of it in 1944. Brooksville Tunnel and its 1928 replacement were destroyed to make way for Interstate Highway 64 in the early 1970s.

Nor do most Blue Ridge Tunnel enthusiasts realize that Brooksville Tunnel was the most dangerous to build of the four. As the *Richmond Daily Dispatch* reported in 1857,

> *Next to the Great Tunnel in point of magnitude, and far exceeding it in the difficulty of its construction, is the Brooksville Tunnel, which passes through a projecting spur of the main mountain, about three miles east of the Great Tunnel…of so treacherous a nature is the rock encountered, that it proved as difficult an undertaking of the sort, as has ever been achieved*

in this country…The slightest disturbance from a blow or a blast would sometimes bring down avalanches of rock into the tunnel, leaving immense cavities above to be filled with packing or propped with timber.[19]

Last, few people know specifics about the men who made Virginia's reach toward the Ohio River possible. Eight hundred Irish famine immigrants—including fifty boys—thirty-one Albemarle County slaves and one hundred local residents built the Blue Ridge Tunnel. They performed this monumental task entirely with black gunpowder and hand tools and without benefit of vertical shafts, pneumatic drills or dynamite. Hundreds more Irish built the other Blue Ridge Railroad tunnels while slaves prepared, finalized and maintained Blue Ridge Railroad track beds. The history of how these laborers came to work on the railroad deserves particular attention.

2

SLAVE LABOR

Blue Ridge Railroad

Four western Albemarle County men leased the labor of black men to the Blue Ridge Railroad: George A. Farrow; his brother-in-law, David Hansborough; their neighbor, Robert P. Smith; and William M. Sclater. The first three were more than country planters looking to monetize slaves they already owned. They were part of a statewide slave-trading network that Claudius Crozet relied on for labor. Sclater, a temporary resident in Albemarle during the railroad construction years, held no slaves in 1850 but was involved with the same network as a slave agent and crew supervisor.[20]

Born in Fauquier County near Washington, D.C., George Farrow worked in adjoining Prince William County as a deputy sheriff and jail handyman during the 1830s and 1840s. Among his duties were mending handcuffs and chains and procuring leg irons. He used the restraints when he jailed black fugitives, including two free runaway women who had been kidnapped and enslaved.[21]

Prince William County is near Washington, D.C., where William Hendricks Williams and his brother, Thomas W. Williams, ran the notorious Yellow House slave pen in the 1840s and 1850s. George Farrow was related by marriage to William U. Barton, a slave scout for the Yellow House pen in 1850 and 1851. Barton was only one thread in a web of rural slave traders who serviced the Yellow House, which, in turn, sent slaves to the urban market in Richmond. In 1847, Thomas W. Williams

The Brooksville house was adjacent to Rockfish Gap Turnpike, now Highway 250. *Distant view*: mountainous terrain where the most difficult construction took place. *Author's collection.*

wrote to slave traders R.H. Dickinson and Brothers in Richmond, stating that he had "six agents out in the country buying…You may look for negroes from me pretty often."[22]

Eager, no doubt, to capitalize on the coming Blue Ridge Railroad project, George Farrow bought 515 acres and a plantation house in Brooksville, a hamlet at the eastern base of Rockfish Gap in Albemarle County, in 1849. When he relocated, he brought along his family and slaves. Two brothers, a sister and her husband, David Hansborough, soon followed. Eight of the twenty-nine black men whose labor Farrow and Hansborough leased for the Blue Ridge Tunnel in 1854 were likely unrelated to the families they held in slavery. Nor did the men share surnames with slaveholding families in Albemarle County. Farrow's Northern Virginia origins and family ties point to William Barton and the Yellow House pen as the point of purchase or leasing of these slaves for railroad work in Albemarle.[23]

In 1850, Robert P. Smith held twenty-five slaves on his property in western Albemarle County. Only six of the male slaves, if we include a fourteen-year-old boy, were the appropriate age for tunnel work. Smith's 1853 promise to Claudius Crozet that he would find a "force of 50 to 60 negroes to work at the Tunnel" if they were paid Irish wages obviously involved more than leasing the labor of slaves who lived on his plantation.[24]

In August 1853, Crozet relayed Robert Smith's offer to the Board of Public Works. Smith would be "in town," or Richmond, Crozet wrote, and "lay the matter before the Board." Richmond was a nexus for the slave trade in the upper South, and at least three firms in the city's slave-trading district specialized in hired labor. Crozet's statement suggests that Smith may have counted on leasing the labor of a large group of black men and then re-leasing them to the Blue Ridge Railroad. Irish floorers at the Blue Ridge Tunnel were earning up to $1.25 a day by August 1853, whereas the hire of a slave on the railroad had been $0.41 a day the year before. Hiring out slaves for Irish wages would substantially increase Smith's profits.[25]

Claudius Crozet also leaned on his manager, William Sclater, for finding slaves as supplements or replacements for Irish laborers. The chief engineer especially wanted Sclater to procure sixty black men in 1854 for preparation of temporary Blue Ridge Railroad tracks. These lay between sections of the Virginia Central Railroad temporary tracks. When all the rails were connected, the mountaintop track, as it was called, would bypass the incomplete Brooksville and Blue Ridge Tunnels and allow rail travel over Rockfish Gap until the full project was completed. Evidence gleaned from seven primary documents proves that Sclater scouted for these slaves and was their general supervisor.[26]

The leased slaves worked at least into early 1855 as they repaired and finalized eight miles of track between Mechum's Depot and Greenwood Tunnel and four detached miles between Greenwood and Rockfish Gap. They broke up rock for ballast and rammed it in, repaired six-story embankments, cleared ditches that had filled with mud during rainstorms, hauled away debris left from mountain slides and probably built fences.[27]

None of Claudius Crozet's slave scouts could deliver the full quota of men he wanted because few planters near the construction or elsewhere in the state would let slaves work near tunnel blasting. George Farrow and David Hansborough provided only two-thirds of the force they wanted to procure for the Blue Ridge Tunnel. Robert P. Smith brought only forty of the fifty men he had promised, and they worked on Blue Ridge Railroad tracks, not in the Blue Ridge Tunnel.[28]

William Sclater gathered only thirty-seven of the requested sixty men for the Blue Ridge Railroad temporary tracks. Most came from Albemarle County slaveholders. These included Alfred D. Mosby, father of John Singleton Mosby

African American railroad laborers in Northern Virginia, circa 1862. *Courtesy of the Library of Congress.*

of Civil War fame, and Socrates Maupin, a University of Virginia physics professor and chairman of the faculty. Tellingly, Thomas W. Williams, co-owner of the Yellow House slave pen, leased the labor of three slaves to William Sclater. Further, the Board of Public Works paid the Williams brothers $143.47 a month to supply provisions for slaves who worked along the line. From the Blue Ridge to the District of Columbia to Richmond and back to the Blue Ridge, the railroad created, in effect, a triangular slave trade. Everyone involved with it, from the governor of Virginia to slave crew overseers, profited from the business of treating human beings as property.[29]

Virginia Central Railroad

No payrolls that might list slaves working on the Virginia Central Railroad have been found, though the 1860 census names thirty-eight black convicts—including three women—who labored for the company in

Alleghany County in the 1850s. Virginia Central's annual reports show that the company routinely hired the labor of more than one hundred slaves each year, with the railroad paying for board, clothing and other provisions. These slaves worked all along the Virginia Central line from Richmond and into Alleghany County.[30]

As to slaves on the Virginia Central's share of the tri-county Blue Ridge Railroad project, the historical record holds few clues. A monthly invoice issued from a Virginia Central depot—possibly Woodville (now Ivy)—shows that four firemen and three hands were working there in 1852. Charles Ellet, chief engineer for the Virginia Central in 1856, maintained the temporary track with the labor of twelve slaves. John S. Cocke, owner of Cocke's Tavern in western Albemarle County, leased the labor of six slaves to the Virginia Central in 1860 and 1861.[31]

Two documents reveal that the Virginia Central Railroad also employed free black men and boys for its portion of the Blue Ridge Railroad project. The same Woodville invoice listed wages of fifteen dollars paid to John, a "free boy." And in 1858, Lewis Harvey, a free man, obtained a judgment in Albemarle County for fifteen dollars of back wages against two men identified in court records as "Mason and Walker." Claiborne Mason was a Virginia Central Railroad contractor for the temporary track in 1854. Reuben Lindsay Walker was a contractor on the west side of Rockfish Gap in 1851.[32]

3

IRISH LABOR

On March 7, 1847, members of the First African Baptist Church in Richmond, Virginia, dressed in Sunday clothes and headed for their house of worship on Broad Street. More than 2,000 members of the congregation were slaves. About 150 were free. A flock that generously gave to charity cases, including Richmond's indigent slaves, they put forty dollars in the penny collection basket for a cause three thousand miles away: the Great Hunger.[33]

This was the year known as Black '47—the peak of the potato blight and famine that lasted in Ireland from 1845 through 1852. On the Sunday that the First African Baptist Church members made their donations, starvation or hunger-related diseases had already decimated much of Ireland's population. The white minister of the church who spoke to the congregants from the pulpit that late winter morning was heeding a call from the Quaker Society of Friends. Its relief committee had met in Washington, D.C., in February, pleading with the nation for donations to an Irish relief fund.[34]

Contributions poured in from around the country. The Choctaw gave $174. A New York rabbi collected $200 from his congregation. The Boston relief committee amassed $150,000 in food and cash. With the approval of Congress, the USS *Jamestown* set sail from Boston for the port city of Queenstown, now Cobh, on the southern coast of County Cork, Ireland, on March 28, 1847. The ship was stuffed with eight hundred tons of food and clothing: 4,889 bags and 705 barrels of cornmeal, 2,043 bags of corn, 1,377 barrels of bread, 413 barrels of beans, 400 barrels of pork, 100 barrels of

Interior of an Irish cabin during the Great Hunger. *Author's collection.*

rice, 100 casks of ham, 88 barrels of peas, 60 barrels of flour, 10 barrels of oatmeal, 85 packages of potatoes, 34 packages of rye, 6 boxes of fish, 4 packages of beans, 3 bags of wheat, 2 packages of oats, 1 cask of dried apples and 32 boxes of clothing.[35]

It was not nearly enough.

When the *Jamestown* arrived in Cork City, the captain found what he described as a "valley of death and pestilence itself. I saw enough in five minutes to horrify me. Hovels crowded with the sick and dying; without floors, without furniture, and with patches of dirty straw covered with still dirtier shreds and patches of humanity…Every corner of the street is filled with pale, careworn creatures, the weak leading and supporting the weaker; women assail you at every turn with famished babies imploring alms."[36]

Paupers in the street meant that no one was plowing fields and reaping harvests to pay rent. By the spring of 1847, English and Anglo-Irish landlords were deeply vexed about their loss of rental income. One landlord, Denis Mahon, lived in a Palladian manor house on a sprawling estate in Strokestown, County Roscommon. He leased thirty thousand surrounding acres from British monarch Queen Victoria. In turn, six thousand Irish men, women and children in twenty-nine townlands were his tenants.[37]

Strokestown House, County Roscommon, circa 1900. The mansion was erected in the 1690s on the former site of a castle belonging to an Irish clan. *Courtesy of Strokestown Park and the Irish National Famine Museum.*

Anxious to rid himself of starving, non-paying renters, Mahon instituted a forced emigration scheme by offering free ship tickets to North America. In May 1847, hundreds of Mahon tenants silently plodded sixty miles east on the road to Dublin and the Liverpool ferry. It was a four-day journey by foot or in a two-wheeled cart. A few days after reaching the miserable docks of Liverpool, they boarded four ships bound for Quebec, Canada. More than half of the exiles died from lack of food or from disease on the voyages. When survivors of the Mahon coffin ships landed, one Canadian doctor observed that they were "without exception, the most wretched, sickly, miserable beings I ever witnessed."[38]

Thousands of tenants still occupied Mahon's leased lands, and more expense was intolerable to him. The townland of Cregga was three miles north of Mahon's mansion. Referring to its residents as a "nest of paupers," he signed one thousand notices in the spring of 1847, giving the tenants of Cregga and other townlands a six-month warning to "deliver up quiet and peaceable possession" of their rented cabins. Mahon's agent began nailing the notices to doors in the Strokestown area on May 1.[39]

Irish emigrants leaving home for America, 1866. *Courtesy of the Library of Congress.*

Losing a house and acreage was disastrous for any Irish farmer. Most of Mahon's tenants stayed put. In November, his agent appeared at their cabins with local Irish police and red-coated English soldiers. They forced occupants from their homes and pounded a staple the size of a horseshoe across the doors to prevent reentry. Hired Irish men called the Crowbar Brigade then knocked down the mud or stone dwellings, sometimes setting the thatched roofs on fire. If pieces of roof survived, evicted tenants dragged away a section, threw it over a ditch and crawled underneath for shelter.

A family of six Fallons—Thomas, Ann, two boys and two girls—were evicted from Cregga. This was likely the same family of Fallons from the Strokestown area who ended up at the Blue Ridge Railroad. Though details of their departure and arrival are unknown, they were living in Staunton, Virginia, by 1851. One of the Fallon daughters married a Blue Ridge Tunnel worker, but neither Thomas nor his two sons appears on any extant Blue Ridge Railroad payroll. The Fallon men may have labored as tracklayers for the Virginia Central Railroad. Between 1846 and 1855, 1.8 million Irish such as the Fallons fled their homeland. Famine immigrants in dire need of employment, they conveniently showed up in time for the westward expansion.[40]

4

CONTRACTORS AND ROAD HANDS

C laudius Crozet's decade-old plan for a railroad line coupling eastern and western Virginia commenced in March 1849 when the state appropriated funds for the Blue Ridge Railroad. The chief engineer established three office-residencies near the coming construction in western Albemarle County. He resided most often at Brooksville in George Farrow's two-story plantation house, which the planter operated as a tavern and inn.[41]

Crozet's residency at Brooksville was useful for both men. Farrow's house was centrally located in the railroad construction zone. In one day on horseback, the engineer could readily check the progress of any point along the Blue Ridge Railroad line. And Farrow, through his frequent contact with Crozet at the inn, had access to the affairs of the railroad—an advantage he used so well through the construction years that he named one of his sons Claudius in honor of his long-term lodger.[42]

Writing from Brooksville on August 18, 1849, Crozet composed an advertisement calling for proposals to build the Blue Ridge and Brooksville Tunnels. He placed the notice in nine newspapers, including the *Baltimore Sun*. The *Irish American Weekly* in New York printed a shorter version.[43] Contractors and laborers from both cities ended up working on the Blue Ridge Railroad. The advertisement stated:

> *TO CONTRACTORS—Blue Ridge Railroad proposals will be received by the undersigned, at his office in Brooksville, Albemarle County, Va. until the 1st of Oct. next, for the construction of the tunnel through the Blue*

Ridge, together with the deep cut and the embankment connected therewith at the end. The tunnel will be 4,260 feet long, 16 feet high and 20 feet wide; with a ditch on each side; it will slope eastwardly at the rate of 65 feet to the mile, and pass 700 feet below the top of the mountain. Proposals will be received either for the whole or for one half, it being distinctly stated, in this case, whether the eastern or western half is bid for. Proposers are requested to examine the localities before bidding, and will obtain from the undersigned all necessary information. The payments will be CASH with a suitable reservation till the completion of the contract. The best testimonials and an energetic prosecution of the work will be expected. Printed forms of the proposal will be furnished on application to the undersigned.

By order of the President and Directors,

C. CROZET,

Engineer Blue Ridge Railroad

Brooksville, Aug. 18, 1849

Proposals will also be received until the 18th of October next, for the Construction of the Railroad, on the Eastern side of the mountain, about eight and a half miles. It comprises much heavy work, and a Tunnel about 750 feet long. C. CROZET, Eng. B.R.R. Co.[44]

Both notices caught the attention of thirty-seven-year-old John Kelly. Born in 1812, likely in the village of Rathcooney, County Cork, Ireland, Kelly was the son of a respectable but small farmer named John Kelly who tilled three acres of rented land north of Cork City. Young John would have attended one of two Catholic schools in the civil parish of Rathcooney, receiving the "rudiments of a plain English education," as a nineteenth-century biography of him stated.[45]

As a teen, Kelly worked in a flour mill. This would have been the extensive Glanmire Flour Mills, located near Rathcooney and next to a river that flowed into the world-class Cork Harbor. Kelly's job became tiresome after a few years. With the sea almost at his doorstep, he must have felt a powerful urge to try his luck elsewhere. He sailed to the United States in 1834 and first found employment on the Long Island–Jamaica Railroad. The following year, he worked on the Baltimore and Susquehanna Railroad. A quick learner and frugal saver, he eventually became a tunnel and bridge builder for the Baltimore and Ohio Railroad under the direction of chief engineer Benjamin Latrobe Jr.[46]

For his Blue Ridge Railroad bid, Kelly garnered a recommendation from James Sykes, member of the Baltimore and Ohio Board of Directors. Sykes certified that Kelly and his nephew, Cornelius, were

A rare image of John Kelly, circa 1873.
Author's collection.

"very industrious, energetick, highminded, honourable men." Kelly enclosed Sykes's letter with a bid for both tunnels while Cornelius sent a more detailed bid one week later. His accompanying cover letter assured Claudius Crozet that he or his uncle could come to Richmond for the letting of the bids. Stock and tools were at the ready, and they could raise as much money as needed for security.[47]

While Crozet waited for all bids to come in, he chose local planter Thomas Jefferson Randolph and his partner, Christopher Valentine, to complete sections seven and eight, or 2.7 miles, of the Blue Ridge Railroad. This portion was sandwiched between Greenwood Tunnel and Blair Park plantation, west of what is now the village of Crozet. Drivers along present-day Blair Park Road in Greenwood, Virginia, can see the rich, rolling farmland of Randolph's sections and the working railroad tracks that still wind around the base of the mountain.[48]

The eldest grandson of Thomas Jefferson, third president of the United States, Randolph was born at Monticello in Albemarle County. After marrying and raising a family there, he and his wife moved to Edgehill Plantation near Shadwell Mills, within view of Monticello Mountain. Randolph was a contractor for the Louisa Railroad in 1849 and had already completed track construction at Shadwell Mills. He enslaved thirty men and boys between the ages of sixteen and fifty-five and probably relied on them to build the Shadwell section—Crozet later wrote that Randolph "worked Negroes altogether." Using stone quarried from the immediate neighborhood, Randolph's crew constructed all of the culverts on the Shadwell Mills section and arched them with brick.[49]

Randolph knew what his black force could accomplish when he completed his proposal for the Blue Ridge Railroad. In addition to masonry walls, he specified box and gothic culverts. A box culvert has a square opening and requires mortared stone. A gothic, or rounded, culvert often requires precisely cut stones assembled in an arch. Clearly, some or all of the Randolph slaves were experienced quarrymen, stonecutters, masons and bricklayers who brought their skills to the Blue Ridge Railroad. Their work was to begin in December 1849, sixty days after the contract was signed. It would be completed by January 1854. The Board of Public Works gave permission for conjugal visits to Edgehill as tracks were finished, stating that "Mssrs Randolph and Valentine contractors on the Blue Ridge Railroad have the privilege of passing free on the cars such hands as may be visiting their wives. Provided the same hands do not go oftener than once in two months and not more than five at one time."[50]

On November 1, 1849, Claudius Crozet contracted sections two, three and four—comprising about two miles of track east of the Blue Ridge Tunnel—to Mordecai Sizer, a twice-widowed contractor from King William County, Virginia. For a sense of these sections, curious travelers can drive up to Rockfish Gap along U.S. Highway 250 West in Albemarle County. Sixty-foot embankments built for the tracks are on the right, or north, side of the road, just before it passes under a railroad bridge. With thirty-two slaves in tow, Mordecai Sizer moved from King William in November, established temporary quarters at George Farrow's Brooksville inn and soon broke ground. Thirty Sizer slaves were men and boys who would have worked on his sections.[51]

On December 1, 1849, John Kelly signed a contract to complete the Brooksville and Greenwood Tunnels. Between the two passages, his predominately Irish force would also build an embankment and culverts at Dove Spring Hollow and slice one hundred feet deep through a stretch that came to be known as Kelly's Cut. Kelly's contract cited the distance as sections five and six. A general view of this area can be seen from the Highway Workers' Memorial overlook on Interstate Highway 64 East in Albemarle County. The steep face of the mountain across the highway gives an idea of the challenge that Kelly's men confronted each day.[52]

Work on John Kelly's sections would begin within sixty days and be completed by January 1853. As it turned out, Thomas Jefferson Randolph's crew finished sections seven and eight ahead of schedule in 1852 while Kelly's men were still laboring on the more rugged five and six sections in 1857.[53]

Page two of John Kelly's boilerplate agreement referred to timber and stone belonging to the railroad after the construction of shanties. Though no stone foundations have been identified along the tracks in sections

Postcard view of Kelly's Cut, just west of Greenwood Tunnel, circa 1898. The cut is two hundred feet long and one hundred feet deep. *Author's collection.*

This postcard view of tracks west of the village of Crozet gives an idea of sections seven and eight on the Blue Ridge Railroad. *Courtesy of the C&O Historical Society.*

five and six, Kelly's Irish laborers probably built numerous shanties for themselves in this mountainous construction area. The shanties would have been small enough to fit on the limited areas of level ground available. Mordecai Sizer's sections were equally sheer and called for the same kind of structure, whereas Thomas Jefferson Randolph's sections were on comparatively flat land. He may have followed the practice of other Virginia railroads, which housed enslaved railroad workers in a single large structure and the overseer in a separate, smaller one.[54]

Much of the planning for the railroad was complete by January 1850, but a critical decision remained. Who would build the Blue Ridge Tunnel? While Irish laborers trickled down from Maryland, Crozet assembled the five lowest bids for the tunnel, designated as section one. Of these, the mid-priced bid was from John Kelly and Company, composed of John Kelly; Irishman John Larguey, who had also worked under Benjamin Latrobe Jr. on the Baltimore and Ohio Railroad; and Christian Detwald, a silent partner. Cornelius Kelly was not included—perhaps his uncle decided he was too young for such a large responsibility. Crozet unwisely chose New Yorker John Rutter, the cheapest bidder at $172,900, to build the Blue Ridge Tunnel.[55]

The comparative estimate for work inside the Blue Ridge Tunnel shows that the Irish needed strong backs as well as skills. It listed excavation of 46,500 cubic yards of rock, one cubic yard being a few inches larger than a standard washing machine. Masonry at the portals called for stone workers who could cut, bevel and place blocks of dressed stone in an arch sixteen feet high. Inside the tunnel, experienced bricklayers would line one half of the ceiling with 1,460,000 million bricks. Approaches to the tunnel required felling trees likely more than one hundred feet tall, digging out the stumps and additional excavation.[56]

Last, the roadbed leading to the east portal would be turned for one-eighth of a mile. Turning the road was a deceptively simple phrase for building a curved embankment that barely clung to the edge of the mountainside. This was vital to Claudius Crozet's design, which called for a perfectly straight passage with daylight visible from end to end. Consequently, a train exiting the east portal in Nelson County would take a sharp left turn on a curve with a narrow radius of 546 feet. The embankment, made of rubble removed after tunnel explosions, would be 135 feet high. As the train chugged out of the darkness, passengers seated on the right side of the cars would look down on a steep chasm, somewhat as if seated on a mountain cable-car gondola.[57]

Numbers belie the grim lives of the men who transformed Crozet's engineering vision into precision-cut reality. Goods that Hugh Crawford, a merchant, offered for sale to contractors and road hands in the *Staunton Spectator* in February 1850 indicate, to an understated degree, the nature of the labor: handsaws and long- and short-handled heavy road shovels. Crawford's "stout stitch downs and extra heavy brogans" were the norm for outdoor winter work, which took place on the Blue Ridge Railroad six days a week and slowed only for frozen ground.[58]

In shanties that the Irish built near both portals of the Blue Ridge Tunnel, families would have used the advertised iron eating utensils and hollow ware metal plates. If we picture the life of a shanty wife, we can see her filling one of Hugh Crawford's tubs at a nearby mountain spring and scrubbing clothes in it. With her newly purchased bucket and broom, she or her children would have cleaned the shanty's wooden or earthen floor. These bare necessities portray subsistence living, if only because the small, bedroom-sized structures could have held little more than straw mattresses, a barrel table and a nail on the wall for hanging clothes.

Shanty life for the black laborers would have been similar yet in all ways overshadowed by enslavement and without the daily comfort of family. Work along the Blue Ridge Railroad was well underway in February 1850 when Joseph Waddell, publisher of the *Spectator*, wrote a commentary on the Fugitive Slave Law then under discussion in state legislatures. It stipulated that anyone helping a fugitive slave in the free states was subject to a stiff fine and imprisonment and that officials who aided in the capture of a runaway would be awarded from five to ten dollars. Waddell advocated that free states pay slaveholders for the value of the runaways and set them free. "We would thus get rid of many troublesome blacks of little value," he wrote, "without encountering the trouble and expense of finding a home for them elsewhere and transporting them thither.[59]

"The disinterested philanthropists of the free States, moreover," Waddell continued, "would soon find themselves surrounded by a pestilent population, and their zeal in the cause of human emancipation would cool down to zero in quick time." Slaves held by Mordecai Sizer and Thomas Jefferson Randolph already had little hope of escaping their forced labor along the tracks. When the Fugitive Slave Law passed in September 1850, the men's chances were reduced, if we borrow Waddell's phrase, to zero.[60]

5

CROZET'S CROWNING EFFORT

On the same day that Joseph Waddell agitated against a pestilent slave population, he noted in his paper the arrival of Irish families in Staunton:

We realized on Saturday last [February 9], *for the first time, that our railroad, about which so much has been said, was not a mere scheme. On that day our streets were quite crowded with Irish laborers brought on to be employed on the work. The rain fell in torrents, but these hardy sons of toil heeded it not and were cheerful and gay as ever. The carts well fitted with luggage, surmounted by the women and children, moved off to their various stations, and in a few days the pick and shovel will be busy along the line.*[61]

The group was made up of Irish from the provinces of Connaught and Ulster. Some found lodgings in a white frame rental house on John Porterfield's farm, located in Tinkling Springs between Waynesboro and Staunton; Virginia Central Railroad contractor O.C. Mulligan had hired them for thirteen miles of track work on this stretch of the line. Word spread that Irish from County Cork who had settled in shanties and rental houses near Waynesboro were planning an attack on the newcomers. The local constabulary ignored the rumor.[62]

Using the same Crowbar Brigade techniques learned firsthand from the British in Ireland, a throng of 250 Corkonian men and women marched through Waynesboro to Tinkling Springs on Monday, February 11, 1850. Many were armed with clubs and pistols. One carried a sword. Ten to

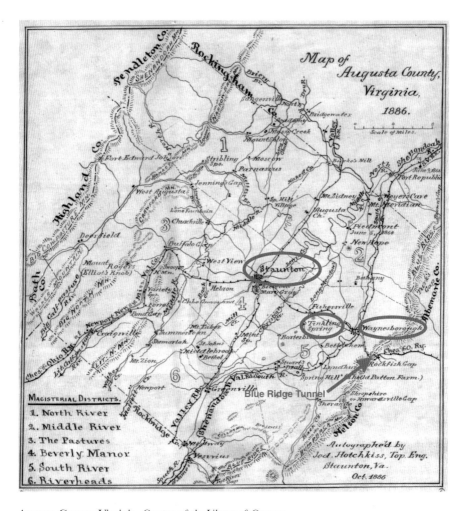

Augusta County, Virginia. *Courtesy of the Library of Congress.*

twelve men and several women occupied the rental house that night. The remaining men were elsewhere, possibly planning a counteroffensive. The *Vindicator* reported that the "Cork-men beat the occupants, broke open their trunks and boxes, tore up and destroyed their clothes, and finally, driving the women into a room and fastening the door, set fire to the house, then took to their heels."[63]

The newspapers reported no injuries, and witnesses identified only fifteen to twenty Corkonians as fomenters of the disturbance, but fifty were arrested on Tuesday, February 12, and jailed in Staunton. They appeared before an examining court composed of five county magistrates. Four prosecutors argued for the commonwealth, while five defense lawyers represented the prisoners. Most of the inmates, but not all, were released three days later. The *Vindicator* noted that fourteen Corkonians were "sent on to await a further trial at the next County Court." In fact, the men numbered fifteen. They remained in jail until their trial on February 26. Six were released on that date, with a June trial date set for the remaining nine men.[64] The *Spectator* accurately reported the cause of the incident:

> *Their mutual animosity is not owing to a difference in religious sentiments, as has been supposed; but it's like the enmity occasioned by feelings of State pride among Americans. The one party or natives of the province of Connaught; the other of Munster, in which is the city of Cork—hence the name Cork-men. Both wish to get the ascendancy on the public works and the stronger invariably drive off the weaker party. A few months ago the Connaught men beat the Cork-men on the road near Cumberland, Maryland, and the dislike of the latter is now embittered by the desire of revenge, which was the immediate cause of the recent outrage in this county. There is a third party, natives of Ulster, called "Far downs," which, we understand, have usually taken part with the Connaught men in their various fights with the Corkonians.[65]*

More recent texts have blamed the disorder on religious differences, while one writer has stated that the Irish "just wanted to have a little fight."[66] Both interpretations are incorrect. Scores of Irish railroad workers and their descendants are buried at Thornrose Cemetery in Staunton, Virginia. Their gravestones are topped with carved crosses rarely used by Protestants in the mid-nineteenth century. The stones and extant marriage records from Saint Francis of Assisi Catholic Church in Staunton prove that most, if not all, Irish on the Blue Ridge Railroad, including men from Ulster, were Catholic. The underlying origins of the riot were sectional differences brought from Ireland that flared along the lines of canal and railroad construction in America at the time. The root of those differences was a desperate need—first in Ireland and then in America—to keep one's job safe from competitors who might accept lower wages or become strikebreakers.[67]

As the nine Corkonians waited in jail across the street from the Augusta County courthouse in Staunton, work began in earnest on approaches to the Blue Ridge Tunnel. By this time, John Rutter had failed to "comply with

Drill holes in the approach to the east portal of the Blue Ridge Tunnel. *Author's collection.*

the terms of his contract," as Crozet later explained to the Board of Public Works. The engineer re-let the tunnel contract to John Kelly and Company.[68]

A *Spectator* article summarized progress at the tunnel and along the line after the author, likely Joseph Waddell, accompanied Claudius Crozet on a tour in March 1850. Thirty hands were working in Augusta County on the Blue Ridge Tunnel's west approach, which was sixty feet long. An additional thirty were working in Nelson County at the east portal approach but had made little progress due to hardness of the rock. Farther east in Albemarle County, Crozet and Waddell came next to Mordecai Sizer's sections two, three and four and then to John Kelly's section five at Dove Spring Hollow.[69]

Waddell pronounced these stretches to be the "most interesting points on the whole road." His description conveys the massive amount of muscled labor taking place:

> *Imagine to yourselves two immense chasms one of 1300 feet and the other of 1000 feet in width—requiring embankments of 80 feet in height. With such declivities, as that the basement will be 160 in width, sidewalls of*

massive masonry, many hundred feet long, and of considerable height, you may have some conception of the great work in these Hollows. At Dove Spring Hollow you are near one of the small tunnels [Brooksville]. Many hands are at work at this point. Considerable progress is made into work preparatory to the commencement of the tunnel. We partook of an excellent dinner at the shantee [sic] of Mr. Kelley, one of the enterprising contractors. If there is any truth in physiognomy, Mr. Kelley has largely developed the traits of a gentleman and much of that frankness and hospitality which are so characteristic of his countrymen.[70]

Waddell ended his piece by proclaiming the project to be "Crozet's crowning effort." Yet his text took no notice of the effort expended by the laborers. With thousands of Irish men and boys toiling on American railroads for low wages, conflict was inevitable. And with the Great Hunger still raging in Ireland, every penny sent home mattered. An announcement in the *Spectator* underscored the need: "Ireland had been relieved by the death and emigration of so large a part of her population, the expenditure for the support of paupers was greatly diminished."[71]

Following the custom of Irish immigrants everywhere, Irish on the Blue Ridge Railroad set aside a generous amount of their earnings. Using the services of Staunton attorney John B. Watts, some groups of workers sent $5 to $100 weekly to Ireland. Others entrusted their money to Waynesboro merchant William Withrow, who conducted the "financial operations of the Irish laborers at the tunnel," the *Spectator* stated, "and indeed on the whole line of the Central Road." Withrow forwarded about $3,500 a year to Ireland. As the workers' agents, both men would have charged a steep fee for writing bills of exchange, a nineteenth-century version of checks. The bills were then transported by ship to correspondents—probably merchants—in Ireland. Distressed recipients collected the funds from the merchants in the form of cash or credit.[72]

The money enabled the chain migration of scores of Irish family members who fled possible death by starvation or disease and joined their relatives on the Blue Ridge Railroad. So laborers on Mordecai Sizer's sections had much at stake when they suspended their work for higher pay in April 1850. Some walked off the job and left the area. The salary of those who stayed remained the same at seventy-five cents a day.[73]

Though the uprising was soon over, it distracted Crozet. He failed to write his quarterly report in April. His May letter to the Board of Public Works caught them up on news of the walkout and detailed current progress on the

Double culvert with yardstick at Robertson's Hollow, western Albemarle County, Virginia. *Courtesy of Paul Collinge.*

railroad. No water had yet interfered with excavation at the west portal of the Blue Ridge Tunnel, but the soft rock encountered might mean arching the entrance sooner than expected as a guard against slides. Water found at the east portal ran down the ravine, posing no obstacle for the time being. Crumbling brown slate was discovered at the east portal but not enough to require a dressed stone arch.[74]

Moving east in his report, Crozet explained that embankments at Robertson's Hollow and Dove Spring Hollow would cover a wide, rapid stream. He outlined his plans for filling the waterway with large rocks and building double culverts to control the flow. Disintegrating rock at the west portal of Brooksville Tunnel was already a problem. Should he arch the entrance for safety now, Crozet asked the board, or wait until later when the work would cost more? Labor on John Kelly's Greenwood Tunnel would soon commence. Thomas Jefferson Randolph had completed one half mile east to Blair Park on his section seven.[75]

Crozet then called the board's attention to the number of hands employed, which totaled 182. "I have directed the contractors to increase their force," he reported, "which could not have been done before, while the cuts were shallow; owing to the impossibility of employing many hands on ground which by its steepness forbids hauling with carts until part of the road bed has been formed for it."[76]

Still more men would be needed when the portals were entered, Crozet explained. Then, he wrote, "hands of a special character must be engaged." The phrase referred to skilled headers and blasters. A two-man team of headers would drill a hole one yard deep in the rock; a blaster would stuff the hole with unstable gunpowder and light the fuse. Executing these jobs in a confined, underground space called for experience, concentration and a dash of fatalism. Both matched well with the qualifications of Irish on the Blue Ridge Railroad. About 60 percent came from mining districts in County Cork and County Kerry, where the men had already learned the perils of underground blasting while mining copper, lead and coal.[77]

Crozet closed his letter by mentioning a dispute with a contractor over an estimate. The contractor was John Kelly, and the engineer's heated quarrel with him was only one of several troubling events that occurred the following month. June 1850 was marred by two violent deaths—the first of many along the Blue Ridge Railroad.

6

AN UNSETTLED MONTH

John Kelly was adamant. His contract for the Blue Ridge Tunnel included building a railroad viaduct over the Rockfish Gap Turnpike, 1,200 feet from the west portal of the passage. Claudius Crozet stoutly denied it. Though Kelly and Company had already quarried stone for the 60-foot-long bridge and had dug 1-foot foundations for abutments earlier in 1850, Crozet argued that Kelly's tunnel contract did not include work more properly considered railroad construction.

Crozet insisted on a separate contract with a lower price for building the viaduct. Kelly refused. When Crozet discussed prices for a separate contract with Kelly's partner, John Larguey, the Frenchman's intolerant temperament encountered obstructive Irish tactics. "John Larguey," a frustrated Crozet reported to the Board of Public Works, "answered 'certainly' a favorite word of his which I have discovered since, implies rather a want of attention to the subject. I repeatedly asked him if he would see Mr. Kelly to which he replied 'certainly' without bringing any answer."[78]

Exasperated, Crozet awarded the contract for the viaduct to the man who would have been his frequent dinner companion at Brooksville: George Farrow. "We feel ourselves aggrieved," Kelly protested to Virginia governor John B. Floyd. "[Our] terms were very considerably below our contract price for that character of work." Farrow paid Kelly for the quarried rock and partly dug foundations, but his quick completion of the viaduct in four months was due to Kelly and Company's prior diggings and a supply of stone already at hand.[79]

By mid-June, laborers were almost ready to blast open portals at two tunnels when the sound of mortal gunfire rang through the hills. The murdered victim was Joseph Marrow, an Irish foreman on Mordecai Sizer's crew. The drunken assailant was Joseph Farrow, also a foreman for Sizer and George Farrow's hotheaded youngest brother. While in his teens, Joseph had been charged with disturbing the peace at a tavern and was indicted for assault. With Mordecai Sizer now in residence at Brooksville, it would have been easy enough for George Farrow to suggest that he hire—and perhaps tame—Joseph, but the position did nothing to help the young man outgrow his temper.[80]

The murder of the Irish man, Crozet wrote to the secretary of the board, "excited all our laborers of that nation to a great degree, they threatening vengeance on two other individuals—yesterday they carried the body for burial to Staunton and will probably return today; Farrow, a brother to the owner of Brooksville, is now in custody in Nelson Co., the occurrence having taken place just across the line. We hope the tremendous excitement of Sunday will subside and that the work will be resumed tomorrow, though Mr. Sizer loses two of his foremen."[81]

A Nelson County court acquitted Joseph Farrow, and George Farrow paid his brother's legal fees. It is unknown if the Irish found their revenge or where they buried Joseph Marrow. He may have been interred in the paupers' section at the newly opened Thornrose Cemetery in Staunton. Marrow's death left five kinfolk, including two small children, to mourn at his grave.[82]

Crozet's priority was avoiding bad publicity. "No doubt the circumstance, though bad enough, will be exaggerated in our papers," he continued in his letter, "and the tunnel will be accounted responsible for the occurrence, as it was for the boy who burned himself by playing with powder." The reference was to two children who had died in May, when a ten-year-old white boy wanted to show a black boy how the Irish worked at the tunnel. The youngster laid a line of gunpowder from a storage facility and lit it. The explosion that followed killed him instantly, while the black child died within hours. To Crozet's dismay, the news appeared in the *Richmond Whig* and other newspapers around the South.[83]

The day after Crozet mailed his letter about the murder, the *Spectator* reported that the jailed Irish rioters who had been awaiting their trial "were discharged for want of evidence against them—the prosecution being abandoned by the attorney for the Commonwealth." It appears that the Irish, though divided by sectional differences, would not testify against their fellow countrymen. The murder of Joseph Marrow may have led them to close ranks, perhaps involuntarily. Fear of retaliation had long been a factor in court cases involving

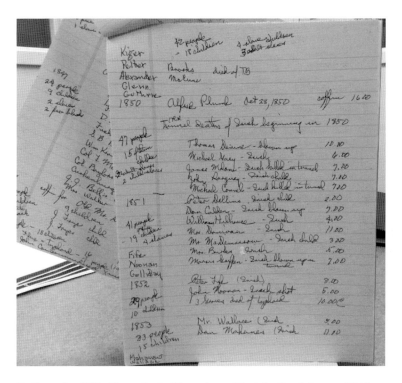

Coffin maker W.B. Alexander in Waynesboro, Virginia, listed deceased Irish and the cost of their coffins for the year 1850. *Transcription by Dorothy Anne Reinbold, courtesy of the Waynesboro, Virginia Public Library.*

Irish workers on American public works projects. "Not one individual of the large body of Irish laborers along the line of the canal dare testify against another of their number in a court of justice," wrote Charles B. Fisk, chief engineer for the Chesapeake and Ohio Canal, in 1836.[84]

The death of Irishman Thomas Devine concluded the disquieting month of June 1850. According to W.B. Alexander, a coffin maker in Waynesboro, Devine was "blown up." The death probably took place at the west portal of the Blue Ridge Tunnel; Devine lived nearby. Though he was the first laborer known to die of an explosion on the Blue Ridge Railroad, Crozet made no note of it in his second annual report to the Board of Public Works.[85]

In the October 5, 1850 report, Crozet listed a number of concerns that were ominous predictors of the future. First, he carefully explained that the height of the mountain at Rockfish Gap prevented the use of vertical work shafts. These would have allowed penetration of the tunnel from above as well as from the sides. He would defend this irrefutable fact often when criticized in the coming years. The engineer knew by now that lack of drainage at the west end of the Blue Ridge Tunnel might be an obstacle, though he could not have predicted that explosions would open unexpected streams of water. He was also aware that the western portal would require a stone arch. But he could not foresee that crumbling, unstable rock would endanger construction at the Brooksville Tunnel for six more years.[86]

Crozet was compelled to ask a second time about the exact location of the western end of the Blue Ridge Railroad: "By whom is the bridge over the South river to be made, and where shall it be? The terminus of the Blue ridge railroad; or, in other words, at what point is it to connect with the line advancing towards it from Staunton?" He explained in his report the critical issues involved—allocation of labor, track placement

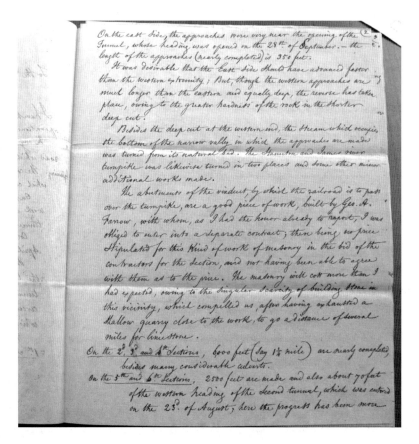

Crozet's October 1850 report mentioned completion of the viaduct, culverts on sections seven and eight and the west heading of Brooksville Tunnel. *Author's collection.*

and the expense of property damages along the route. Likewise, Crozet pointed out, the Blue Ridge Railroad was of no use until the board and the Virginia Central Railroad decided which entity would fund tracks from Mechum's River to Blair Park on the east side of Rockfish Gap. With no direction as yet on these issues, the chief engineer's ability to direct the complex Blue Ridge Railroad project was hobbled.[87]

Crozet also complained about the scarcity of easily worked stone for culverts. The shortage would hinder his contractors for the next seven years. More interesting now is the question of who built the culverts, as some are visible and many are still in use. On the east side of Rockfish Gap, we have seen that Thomas Jefferson Randolph's black crew possessed the skills to build the fifteen culverts between Greenwood Tunnel and Blair Park. Brooksville Tunnel payrolls indicate that Irish and local stonemasons would have constructed the cement-sealed, double gothic culverts—five and a half feet wide each and eight and a half feet high—at Dove Spring Hollow. Mordecai Sizer's force built double box culverts and "many considerable" more, as Crozet wrote, at Robertson's Hollow and Goodloe Hollow, the ravine just west of it. We do not know who directed the work. In the

Gothic culvert on the western slope of Rockfish Gap. *Courtesy of Paul Collinge.*

Interior of gothic culvert. Height and width, including piers, is seven feet. *Courtesy of Paul Collinge.*

Bluegrass region of antebellum Kentucky, Irish masons oversaw the labor of slaves who learned their skills as apprentices on the job. If this were the case with Sizer, it may explain why he used a varying mixed-race crew, now swollen, Crozet reported, to "140 hands, mostly negroes."[88]

The most visually impressive culvert on the Blue Ridge Railroad lies near the bottom of the western slope of Rockfish Gap. A gothic culvert with an inscribed keystone, it is downhill from George Farrow's viaduct, which is now a pile of rubble. Two local and five Irish masons, including master Irish mason Peter Crowe from County Clare, worked on the viaduct. Any of them might have carved the Freemason T-square and compass on the keystone, but traditionally that honor went to the one who had achieved master status. In this case, it would have been Peter Crowe, whose skills Claudius Crozet so respected that he occasionally gave direct orders for the mason's services elsewhere on the railroad.[89]

A GREAT AMOUNT OF LABOR

Claudius Crozet's January 1851 letter to the Board of Public Works opened on an optimistic note. Since October 1850, work had "progressed all along with the same spirit," he reported. Only a short interruption on sections contracted to Mordecai Sizer and Thomas Jefferson Randolph slowed progress. The work stoppage may have been due to permitting the slaves a brief Christmas break with their families. Operations soon resumed, and Crozet was pleased that Randolph had increased his force. Randolph's partner had been seeking hired slaves for their sections. By this time, he may have contracted additional black laborers from local slaveholders.[90]

Crozet's problem now was convincing the board that the railroad had advanced as well as could be expected. The Richmond gentlemen were uncomfortably aware that laborers at Kingwood Tunnel on the Baltimore and Ohio Railroad near Wheeling, Virginia, had blasted through 2,100 feet in seven months, or 300 feet a month. Crozet admitted that only 178 feet, or 36 feet a month, had been removed from the west side of the Blue Ridge Tunnel. He soothed the board's anxieties by explaining that Kingwood had three vertical work shafts. Laborers there could assault the mountain from two horizontal headings at the east and west sides, just as at the Blue Ridge Tunnel. But they had the additional advantage of blasting at both sides of each vertical shaft, for a total of eight attack points. The mountain at Rockfish Gap, Crozet clarified again, was too "high and steep" for vertical shafts.[91]

The chief engineer further explained that night shifts at Kingwood doubled the work time. When a sufficient amount of excavated material

A cart track at an unidentified cut. *Author's collection.*

was removed from the west heading of the Blue Ridge Tunnel, a cart track would be extended into the passage. Night shifts could then commence, and sixty to seventy feet of progress a month would be the norm. Even without night shifts, Crozet assured the board, advancement at the west portal spoke "favorably of the energy of the contractor, Mr. Larguey, who conducts the operations."[92]

In the absence of first-person accounts, we cannot know what the Irish thought of night work. When writing to the board about three consecutive eight-hour shifts at the Blue Ridge Tunnel, Crozet noted that the hours of labor were "as important to the men as its price." This could mean that the Irish were eager for multiple wage-producing shifts. Irish canal workers of the time offer an alternate view. For those who had been farmers in Ireland before the Great Hunger, night shifts were an industrial clock imposed on an agrarian, sunup-to-sundown working day. For example, Jeremiah Crowley was a laborer on the Chesapeake and Ohio Canal Company's Paw Paw Tunnel in 1849. He toiled as a floorer in the Blue Ridge Tunnel from 1853 to 1857. He would have been familiar with night shifts at the Paw Paw and with protests from fellow Irishmen there, one of whom complained, "They give twenty-one minutes to eat…scream, threaten, and shout at you, while forcing you back to work."[93]

Night shifts were already in place at the east portal, where the hard greenstone was a perennial problem. The opening had a "fine appearance," Crozet wrote. But though the work carried on "without interruption, day and night," the men blasted away only nineteen feet a month. Crozet pointed out that tunneling was an inexact business, adding, "All I can say with certainty about it is that the contractor [John Kelly] is alive to his interest and remarkably energetic and skillful in this business."[94]

Though the issue of who would build from Mechum's River to Blair Park in Albemarle County still hampered Crozet's plans, the question of the western terminus of the Virginia Central Railroad was resolved by January 1851. The Blue Ridge Railroad would build the South River Bridge at the bottom of the western slope of Rockfish Gap. The Virginia Central would push beyond Staunton and lay tracks to Covington in Alleghany County—construction that eventually included four more tunnels. The decision meant that Crozet would have to link with Virginia Central tracks sooner than expected, but he could proceed on the west side at last.[95]

Crozet now altered his strategy of finishing the Blue Ridge Tunnel before contracting the three miles down the western slope. He invited bids for four sections. Section nine, or one mile, began at the end of the approach to the west portal. Sections ten and eleven proceeded two miles down the slope. Section twelve was the South River Bridge. The chief engineer accepted a bid for all four sections from Reuben Lindsay Walker, a civil engineer and graduate of Virginia Military Institute, and Hugh Gallaher, an experienced canal builder and first-generation Irish American.[96]

The two contractors used slave and Irish labor on the western slope, but the cost of both was rising. Slave labor increased from $125 a year per man to $130 in 1851. Irish working on these sections threatened a strike after Irishmen Don Calden and Morris Griffin were blown up in the Blue Ridge Tunnel in January 1851. The threat worked. Irish wages rose from $0.75 to $0.87½ a day early in the year. On March 1, pay increased to $1.00 a day.[97]

Kelly and Company, realizing that the Blue Ridge Tunnel would take much longer than expected, negotiated a new agreement that the Board of Public Works finalized in December 1851. It would complete the passage and one thousand feet beyond the east portal, but the state must cover all expenses and pay them 10 percent of the estimated cost of $200,000. Kelly and Company would reduce its final fee by 2 percent of costs exceeding $200,000. Christian Detwald, its early partner, dropped out of the enterprise at this point.[98]

Kelly and Company's ledger for construction expenses began with the new contract. Two hundred kegs of blasting powder and one thousand feet of safety fuse were the first purchases listed. These would have been delivered to a company store or staging area near the Blue Ridge Tunnel. The contractors replenished supplies of fuse every month, along with hundreds of matches. Safety fuse, invented by Englishman William Bickford in 1831, consisted of a tube of woven jute filled with powder and sealed with tar. It burned at the predictable rate of one foot per second, giving nearby men enough time to dash from the area. Safety fuse was a vast improvement over its predecessor, which was a powder-filled quill or length of straw that burned at a random rate. Still, even with safety fuse, a stray spark from a match could cause an early explosion. This was the likely cause of death for Don Calden and Morris Griffin.[99]

MARY JANE BOGGS WAS an enthusiastic eighteen-year-old lover of mountains. She kept a journal when she, her father and two cousins journeyed by wagon and buggy over Rockfish Gap, Virginia, in June 1851. Through her eyes, we can experience pre-train travel and take a rare look at the railroad construction.

The family left Spotsylvania County very early in the morning. Their luggage and a tin cup for drinking water were strapped to the back of the wagon. After passing through Charlottesville, the family traveled west on the Rockfish Gap Turnpike. "We…stopped to take dinner at Brooksville, at a tavern or I should say a 'Hotel' kept by Mr. Farrow," Mary Jane wrote with a minute script in her four- by five-inch diary. "Father had told me that Brooksville was a pleasant place, but I was surprised to see the parlor so handsomely furnished; an elegant piano, a table covered with prettily bound books, nice curtains, mantel ornaments etc. The accommodations at Brooksville are very good & the scenery around it wild & at the same time beautiful."[100]

Mary Jane could not have known that Brooksville was a prime example of how cheap Irish labor and free slave labor used for the railroad were boosting the area's economy. Six family groups of forty-three slaves lived in nine houses on the plantation.[101] Five men from these family groups would work in the Blue Ridge Tunnel in 1854. While Mary Jane rested in an upstairs room before dinner, field hands from the same slave families tended the oat crop that George Farrow would store over the coming winter and sell to the railroad.[102]

A boardinghouse that Farrow probably rented to fifty-four Irish laborers and family members stood a few yards west of the inn. A second nearby dwelling housed four Irish while a third housed eleven more. If Farrow owned these houses, he enjoyed rental income from the Irish throughout the railroad construction years, as well as lodging fees from railroad personnel. Between 1850 and 1860, a steady stream of contractors and engineers roomed at the inn. They would have paid their rent out of pocket, as did Claudius Crozet, with Brooksville slaves providing all services. A cemetery with unadorned fieldstones lay one-half mile behind George Farrow's house. Some of the stones marked the anonymous graves of Irish railroad casualties, and perhaps slaves, who died while contributing to his prosperity.[103]

Quicker access by rail to markets in Richmond increased the number of retailers in Charlottesville and raised real estate prices. Albemarle County planters saw their land value rise by more than a third in the 1850s. George Farrow did particularly well. In 1850, the cash value of his land was $20,000. It rose to $48,000 by 1860. Direct commerce with the railroad was another bonus. Farrow was one of ninety-three in-state vendors—most of them local planters—for the Blue Ridge Railroad. In addition to oats, he and his brothers sold rope, mules and other supplies to the railroad, transporting them to construction sites in exchange for hauling fees. Brooksville Plantation grew from 515 acres to 1,552 by 1862. Farrow's slaveholdings increased by ten. The Civil War would leave the planter with only his elegant piano and

View from Interstate Highway 64 East. Highway 250 just below the overlook follows, somewhat, the old Rockfish Gap Turnpike route that Mary Jane Boggs traveled. *Author's collection.*

a pocket watch as taxable personal property. For now, though, his coffers were full.[104]

The Boggs family left Brooksville in late afternoon, setting off in a light rain. The road they followed up to Rockfish Gap "wound along the side of the mountains," Mary Jane wrote, "so as not to give the idea of a steep ascent."[105] Only short stretches of this byway remain, but a similar view of her description can be seen from the first and highest overlook after crossing Rockfish Gap on Interstate Highway 64 East. Also gone are the Irish shanties she saw on both sides of Rockfish Gap:

> *I was indebted to an Irishman for one of the prettiest views of the Valley. One of the poor men who work on the railroad had made a clearing among the trees in order to plant his potatoes. There are a great many Irish cabins on each side of the mountains, which reminded me of descriptions I have read of the manner of living of the lowest class in Ireland. They are mere hovels, & most of them have one or two barrels on top of the chimney, but in some of them, we saw muslin curtains, a strange mixture of dirt &*

finery. The people are real Irish wretched, miserable & dirty in appearance, but they hold on to Irish fun & Irish potatoes, as well as Irish tempers. Father called to a man who was at the door of one of the cabins & told him he had often seen double barreled guns but had never before heard of double barreled chimnies, and he seemed very much pleased.[106]

Mary Jane's account of the shanty settlements is packed with evidence of how the Irish would have felt about their dwellings. Her words tell us that the cabins were the equivalent of Class 4 housing—the lowest designation—in Ireland. Those lodgings had mud or timber walls, thatched roofs, one or two rooms and one or no window. The timber shanties at Rockfish Gap would have seemed familiar to Irish workers who had been landless laborers in Ireland. For Irish farmers forced by the Great Hunger to abandon their Class 3 or Class 2 dwellings with brick walls and two or more rooms, the shanties were a mean comedown.[107]

We last see the Boggs family after they have crossed the mountain at Rockfish Gap, their vehicles bumping down the western slope. The late June light was waning, and beds awaited them at a Waynesboro hotel. "We had not time to go down to the mouth of the tunnel," Mary Jane wrote. "It is a stupendous undertaking, & will require a great amount of labor to complete it. Some of the embankments & deep cuts of the railroad too must have required a great deal. We passed under an arch composed of mason work over which the railroad is carried. It was built under the supervision of a man named Farrow & his name & that of Colonel Crozet, a celebrated engineer on that road are inscribed on the inside."[108]

Mary Jane seemed unaware that George Farrow, owner of the inn where she had just eaten a meal, was the same man whose name she saw carved on the viaduct arch. Nor did she realize that Claudius Crozet resided at the same inn, possibly on the second story, where she had recently rested. But that she was well aware of Crozet's renown as chief engineer for the Blue Ridge Railroad emphasizes how essential he and the project were to the people of Virginia.

As the Boggs family continued their summer holiday in 1851, two Virginia Central Railroad contractors nudged the railroad five miles west from Charlottesville to Woodville. Mechum's River, three miles west of Woodville, was their final goal. The contractors were Wright and Farish, first names unknown. Tracks were completed to Mechum's River by March 1852, though the depot there was still under construction and not ready for passengers. An invoice submitted by the Woodville stationmaster to

Crossing Mechum's River Bridge, 2011. *Courtesy of the C&O Historical Society.*

the Virginia Central Railroad that month reflects significant commercial activity. Barrels of steel and loads of sand, coal and iron crossed the bridge at Woodville. All of it was then hauled by wagon farther west for the railroad construction. The Virginia Central invoice serves as a sort of payroll. It named three train hands and listed their total weekly wages of twelve dollars. Four firemen earned a total of seventeen dollars a week. We can assume these men were slaves because the stationmaster wrote only their first names, as was often the custom. He listed no wages for seventeen unnamed depot hands and five unnamed yard hands. They may have been Irish workers whom the contractors paid directly. Weekly board for all the men was one dollar each.[109]

This single invoice tells us little about pay arrangements for the Virginia Central Railroad portion of the Blue Ridge Railroad project. Payrolls for the Blue Ridge Tunnel reveal much more about Blue Ridge Railroad wages. Though extant payrolls do not begin until April 1852, we can assume that men and boys who worked steadily at the tunnel from 1852 through 1857 were likely there from the beginning of construction in 1850. The payrolls show that men often worked two different jobs or labored on both sides of the mountain within the same pay period, which ended on the twenty-sixth of the month. Only pay rates, no jobs, were

A Sportsman passenger train heading east to Ivy (formerly Woodville), Virginia, 1958. *Courtesy of the C&O Historical Society.*

listed for the boys. Wages for the same job performed by different men varied within any particular month.[110]

A second snapshot of wages on the Blue Ridge Railroad comes from a list of expenses that a Waynesboro brick maker submitted to Claudius Crozet in June 1852. The bill for burning 167,900 bricks listed wages for hired hands and the board of white men, "negroes" and white boys. The document is also helpful because it designates a boy as being from twelve to sixteen years of age and gives a fourth example of a mixed-race crew working on the Blue Ridge Railroad.[111]

In the spring of 1852, Mordecai Sizer's crews partially completed section four east of the Blue Ridge Railroad. The work called for a high embankment across the ravine at Robertson's Hollow. To form the embankment, Sizer's men would have used techniques similar to those on canal construction, whereby wheelbarrow men wore metal cleats for stabilization as they rolled barrows on planks leading to the edge of the fill. By the time the embankment was finished, Sizer's men had excavated and moved 38,272 cubic yards of earth and rock from a cut in the mountain. Crozet was familiar with sliding earth in the Allegheny Mountains. But he had never seen it east of the Blue Ridge and lamented the frequent slides on Sizer's section. To see the laws of

Mordecai Sizer's cash box. *Courtesy of Betty Gwathmey and Steve Elder.*

physics undo the work of men must have discouraged everyone, especially the laborers, who had to put things right again. Sizer fled the Blue Ridge Railroad as soon as possible that spring. He transferred remaining work at Robertson Hollow to contractors Hugh Gallaher and Samuel McElroy and wed his third wife in Richmond.[112]

While laborers pressed ahead in the summer of 1852, Claudius Crozet contracted with a worker named Paul Stevens to build a ventilation system for the Blue Ridge Tunnel. The device would remove clouds of smoke after black powder explosions by forcing it out through pipes. Stevens hired eight local men in August and September to build the sorely needed machine; they worked on the west side. As this was their only employment in the passage, they had earned no seniority. Yet their pay was from $1.50 to $1.75 a day. The high wages would be a factor in the coming 1853 strike.[113]

The year of 1852 ended on a high note when the depot at Mechum's River opened on December 6. The rails now provided an unbroken route of 107 miles from Richmond to a point 8 miles west of Charlottesville. This was the end of the line. Passengers arriving at Mechum's River switched to stagecoaches for the remainder of the trip over the mountain. The Blue

Ridge Railroad was far from complete, and portage of goods on the turnpike across the mountain was still necessary, but merchants and farmers west of Rockfish Gap took immediate advantage of the finished tracks. Freight traffic heading east from Augusta County tripled between October 1851 and October 1852. It was merely the beginning of an onslaught of commerce that, thanks to the coming temporary track, would move back and forth across the hazy Blue Ridge long before the main tunnel was finished. Though the track would mollify an impatient public, Claudius Crozet struggled with changes that called for his cooperation with an equally intolerant chief engineer.[114]

A VERY TRYING TIME

Claudius Crozet had projected 1853 as the completion year for the Blue Ridge Tunnel. But in April of that year, it was clear that he was wildly off mark. Alarmed, the Virginia Central Railroad hired Charles Ellet as chief engineer of its company. Ellet had been chief engineer for the James River and Kanawha Canal from 1836 to 1838. In 1842, he designed and built the first wire suspension bridge in the United States. This was followed by the country's longest suspension bridge at Wheeling, Virginia, in 1848. A strong ego accompanied Ellet's success. "They say your temper is too dictatorial," his wife admonished him after the James River Canal Company fired him in 1838. "Everyone gives you credit for talent of the highest order, but many think your disposition overbearing in the extreme."[115]

Charles Ellet brought a good measure of his authoritarian manner to the new position. He immediately assessed progress of the "state work," as he called the Blue Ridge Railroad, and found it wanting. By his estimate, the Blue Ridge Tunnel would not be finished for three years, leaving a mountain gap that only stagecoaches and wagons could traverse. This meant a significant loss of passenger and freight income for Virginia Central Railroad stockholders. Reporting back to the company's directors, he firmly stated that the "Blue Mountain should be crossed by the cars immediately, with a tunnel or without a tunnel."[116]

Ellet's solution was a temporary railroad. East to west, plans for the track initially consisted of running straight through Kelly's Cut, despite Claudius Crozet's objection that progress there would be halted. Ellet prevailed; a temporary track around Kelly's Cut was not completed for two years. Three half-circles of track would follow Kelly's Cut. The first, about one-half mile in length, would wind south of the unfinished Brooksville Tunnel. The second, about three-quarters of a mile, would pass around precarious embankments at Robertson and Goodloe Hollows. The final section of the detour would curve 4.4 miles, with switchbacks, over the mountaintop and down the western slope for 450 feet.[117]

After approval from the Virginia Central's directors, Ellet quickly gathered his own labor force and contractors, made surveys and prepared general plans. He completed these arrangements, he later wrote, "before the contractors reached the ground with their men." The speed of the decision caught Crozet "unawares," as he told the Board of Public Works, though he tried to accommodate the modifications. Two of Crozet's loyal assistant engineers left the Blue Ridge Railroad in April 1853. Ellet replaced them with his own assistant that same month. An abrupt construction change was also necessary. The intended cut through Goodloe Hollow, just west of Robertson's Hollow, would take too long. Instead, Crozet directed contractors Hugh Gallaher and Samuel McElroy to build a one-hundred-foot-long tunnel on the section they had inherited from Mordecai Sizer. Crozet variously referred to this passage as the little, short and small tunnel.[118]

The temporary track meant that Blue Ridge Railroad contractors now had two bosses and twice the pressure to finish their sections. Only one of them let Charles Ellet direct his work while John Kelly rejected Ellet's offer outright. "Mr. Kelly certainly will not permit it," Ellet told Crozet. At least the future temporary track put to rest Crozet's three-year-old worry when the Blue Ridge Railroad assumed responsibility for rails between Mechum's River and Blair Park. Tracklayer N.S. Carpenter paid the fare from Richmond for his Irish hands and supervised their laying of tracks on this section.[119]

Charles Ellet later noted, "Construction was commenced at a period when there was a most unusual demand for labor, and it was extremely difficult to procure an adequate supply." Irish workers on the Blue Ridge Railroad realized that a shortage of laborers for the temporary track would give them clout if they demanded a raise. Added to this was a lingering resentment over the treatment of a floorer injured at the Blue Ridge Tunnel in December 1852. When a blast ripped off the hands of Michael Curran, the Blue Ridge Railroad paid his full salary of one dollar a day in January 1853 but suspended pay in February. In March, John Kelly asked that his wages continue. The Richmond men replied, "The Board have no authority to apply the public funds in the manner desired."[120]

East portal of Little Rock Tunnel. *Courtesy of the C&O Historical Society.*

Just as the Irish swore vengeance when Joseph Marrow was murdered in 1850, they must have been equally angered on behalf of their injured fellow laborer. The volatile situation was made worse by the loss of two Cork men working at the Blue Ridge Tunnel. According to death records, one of them died in the Augusta County poorhouse "from a hurt on the railroad" on April 8. Dan Sullivan's injury from what cemetery records stated was an "accidental sliding of earth" at the tunnel was the tipping point. Sullivan died around April 16. He was buried on April 19. The Irish would have attended the wake and funeral in Staunton, returned to Rockfish Gap and laid out their demands; payrolls show that almost all men on both sides of the tunnel stopped work by that date.[121]

On the same day, Crozet relayed news of the strike to the board. Ignoring Dan Sullivan's death, he blamed it on Paul Stevens, the man he had hired to build the ventilation apparatus. "While engaged at the Tunnel," Crozet wrote, "I am told that he tampered with the hands, telling them that they did not receive enough, that $1.50 per day was the price for working in a Tunnel etc."[122]

Stevens, who had already abandoned his work on the ventilation machine, left for Cincinnati, Ohio. He then urged men at the Blue Ridge Tunnel to join him because they could excavate a tunnel there for $1.50 a day. The workers "adopted $1.50 as their due in the heading," wrote Crozet, "and struck immediately."[123]

Four strikers with the same surname as contractor John Larguey lived in his house on the west flank of Rockfish Gap. Family ties were strong among the Irish. Larguey sided with his kinsmen. He was willing to pay headers $1.50 at the heading and floorers $1.25 in the bottom, saying, "The Tunnel is long, smoky and wet." But Crozet stood his ground. "If, at last, we have to go up so high," he told the board, "let it be with new comers, who have not been guilty of embarrassing us and stopping work without warning."[124]

The chief engineer advised the board to advertise for two hundred strikebreakers in Baltimore, Philadelphia, New York and Boston newspapers. "I suggest a good deal of trouble for you," he acknowledged, "but this is an important crisis, and I agree with Kelly not Larguey, that concessions will be ruinous…We hold in our hands, as it were, the fate of the System of improvements; were it for the Tunnel alone, I would incline to yield, but the consequences to other works frighten me."[125]

The other works included the Covington and Ohio Railroad. First surveyed in 1850 and chartered by the state in February 1853, it was the final, northwestern link for the continuous line from Richmond to the Ohio River. Construction had already begun. Charles Ellet was making plans, as well, for the first of Virginia Central's four tunnels beyond Staunton. He would soon let the contract. A labor shortage on the three Virginia railroads hurrying toward the Ohio River would be a crisis, indeed. Following his own advice to the board, Crozet composed an advertisement that ran for one month in the *Richmond Daily Dispatch*: "Two hundred men will find employment on the Blue Ridge Railroad and Tunnel, in Virginia, where liberal wages will be paid them."[126]

When the notice failed to attract laborers, Father Daniel Downey, pastor of Saint Francis of Assisi Catholic Church in Staunton, Virginia, stepped in. Born in 1800 in Downpatrick, County Down, Ireland, and ordained at

Maynooth College, Downey made the rounds of seven Catholic missions in Virginia. One of them was a wooden plank chapel that the Irish erected on the mountain at Rockfish Gap for his monthly visit. Despite heavy pastoral duties and a threat of violence from Corkonian strikers, the Ulster priest was able to resolve the three-week-long walkout with a compromise. Headers' pay rose to $1.25 a day while floorers received $1.12½. Blasters and headers in the dangerous center of the tunnel earned $1.50. The men were back at work by May 1.[127]

Crozet summarized post-strike news for the board:

> *Though the Tunnel was soon filled again, it was, in a great measure at the expense of the outside works. The men who went away, as I understand, have been deceived; and, if I am rightly informed, this occasioned a later strike in Cincinnati of three weeks duration, which ended in their getting $1.25 per day in the Tunnel heading, just what they might have had here. The strike was marked with circumstances of such a lawless character, that concessions were impossible.*[128]

It is unclear which strike was marked with lawless character. Crozet may have been referring to a threat that a striker posted on a blacksmith's shed on the west side of the Blue Ridge Tunnel: "Let no man go to work in this Tunnel without a dollar and a half in the heading and dollar and twenty-five cents in Bottom; take notice, young or old, married or unmarried, let them look out for shanty powder & ball."[129]

With construction of the temporary railroad well underway, the board could ill afford another work stoppage. The *Daily Dispatch* reported that board members approved a resolution on July 11, 1853, for the hire of the maximum number of workers for the Blue Ridge Railroad, which, the paper stated, "is a work of great magnitude and difficulty." The Richmond men's irritation showed in the humiliating public requirement that Crozet "should make to the Board a daily report of the progress and condition of the work, and the number of hands employed."[130]

How well Crozet fulfilled the board's demand for daily proof of progress is unknown, but his need to produce written evidence of competence was apparent in his August 1853 report: "I have also caused to be prepared an extract from the check roll showing that there has always been a full complement in the Tunnel, except in April last [1853], at the time of the Strike."[131]

In the same letter, Crozet claimed that Irish spendthrifts were causing the labor shortage. "Every day," he fretted, "some of the men fail to go to work, an evil without a remedy that I could suggest; and which is likely to increase, with the improvident, as wages rise. Before the present year, we had numerous applications for work and could enforce discipline: But now, those men must be taken on their own terms, or else they will leave without ceremony."[132]

Blue Ridge Tunnel payrolls show that the men knew they were not machines. Their modest wage increase after the strike gave them enough leeway for two consecutive days of rest or the choice of working only day shifts. Of men on the east side of the tunnel, 15 percent did precisely that, especially the floorers. For them, a single shift meant eight hours of loading sizeable rocks into carts and then unloading them outside the tunnel. The remaining 85 percent of men on the July 1853 payroll worked the full twenty-two days of the payroll period or close to it. Irish at the Blue Ridge Tunnel also needed time off for injury, family illness, wakes and funerals. In 1853, disease carried away five children. Three women died, one from grief, as stated on the death record. In all, eight men died at the tunnel that year, including a floorer who fractured his skull in June.[133]

Numerous days off and multiple deaths meant that labor was scarcer than ever. Crozet set himself the task of inventing a siphon that would free up manpower by automating the pumps. The west portal of the Blue Ridge Tunnel was fifty-seven feet higher than the east. Poor drainage meant that men at the west end sloshed in water as they worked. "The water also has become suddenly very troublesome," Crozet told the board, "but I expect that the large siphon I am erecting will relieve us from that difficulty; and besides, save several men, a most important consideration at this juncture."[134]

Crozet considered his siphon invention an experiment. Should it fail, he was willing to share the pipes with the Virginia Central Railroad, which needed them.[135] He described the siphon as

2,000 feet long and 3 inches in diameter, it being the longest siphon on record. I was afraid of trying pipes of a larger diameter, on account of the greater quantity of air that would be disengaged at the apex, and cause the siphon to be fed too often. The siphon has perplexed us with singular phenomena, and we have not yet been able to make it work constantly. It has to be fed every half hour through the air vessel, and must be fed fully every 12 hours on its whole length. Still it discharges about 60 gallons per minute, which is a valuable assistance.[136]

In fact, the siphon—made of 9-foot-long, cast-iron pipes—was 1,792 feet in length. Initially, Crozet applied oakum and pitch caulking to the pipe

Drainage ditches at the abandoned Blue Ridge Tunnel east portal silted in, creating a water problem until construction of a rail-to-trail path in 2015. *Author's collection.*

connections. Too porous, these substances allowed the entrance of air. Though he switched to joint putty made of lead, varnish and boiled linseed oil, the mixture only partly alleviated the problem.[137]

The summit of the siphon was nine feet above the pooled water. The end was twenty feet below it. The idea was to force water up and out of the passage, but the very length of the siphon prevented it. Air immediately separated from the water, backed up to the head of the siphon and acted as a plug that stopped the flow. The siphon never functioned as well as needed, and though it released some laborers from the pumps so they could work elsewhere, the gain was insignificant.[138]

In his August 1853 report, Crozet explained that he, Charles Ellet and Claiborne Mason, a contractor for the Virginia Central temporary track, were looking for additional workers. "This is a very trying time, to myself especially," the beleaguered Crozet wrote, "as I hold a position which is the key to a long line of operations; and public impatience does not stop to inquire into causes; results are all it is willing to know."[139]

The labor shortage crimped progress all along the Blue Ridge Railroad line. At Crozet's urging, N.S. Carpenter's Irish tracklayers were rapidly laying four miles of rail between Mechum's River and Blair Park on the east side of the project. But a sliding embankment near the river at Lickinghole Creek was a nettlesome problem. Crozet suspended work at the South River Bridge on the west side of the mountain and redirected hands so they could raise the embankment. Stretching his manpower further, Crozet hired Waynesboro mechanic William Crouse to produce the ventilation machine. As part of the agreement, Crouse was also at the ready to help supervise construction of the newly planned little tunnel west of Robertson's Hollow.

Labor was only one difficulty that troubled Crozet in 1853. He was deeply worried about the safety of rails that he must soon turn over to the Virginia Central. Blue Ridge Railroad embankments were still "green," as he put it. The earth had not yet settled. The cross ties would be unstable until after winter weather froze, the ground thawed and the ties were tamped down again. The west slope was particularly unsound. "I conceive it my duty to give the warning," he told the Board of Public Works, "the most watchful precautions will be required here for a long time." The chief engineer was so concerned about the west slope that he reduced the radius of the curves to a minimum of 819 feet because, he wrote, "trains going rapidly down such an incline and pressing hard against curves, together with the rocking consequent upon irregular & considerable settling, will be in great danger of breaking axles, springs, or wheels, or jumping the rail."[140]

Crozet had specified rails that were fifty-nine pounds to the running yard in weight. These were safer for "heavy grades and short curves," he told the board. Charles Ellet insisted on sixty-three pounds to the running yard. Though the change was not Crozet's preference, the rails had to match those of the Virginia Central Railroad, and public pressure for the temporary track gave him little time for argument. "Seeing that this is ultimately to be the work of the [Virginia Central Railroad] company," Crozet told the board, "I cannot see any great objection to the substitution." But he was as unyielding as possible about ballast, the coarse stone that would stabilize the rails. "Ballasting," he explained, "seems indispensable on strong grades, especially with short curves, to keep the track from sliding forward or being pushed outward, by rapid & heavy engines, going down reversed & with breaks down; producing thus an enormous amount of horizontal & lateral friction tending to shove the track out of place."[141]

Though Crozet postponed ballasting on two embankments until spring, after the earth settled, he reluctantly applied it to other portions of the Blue Ridge Railroad. "In thus hastening the completion of this [temporary] portion of the road," he wrote, "I have consulted the public wish more than my own judgment, which would be against laying the track before at least one winter has passed over every part of the road."[142]

By the fall of 1853, Crozet could look back with satisfaction at completed parts of the project. Some of N.S. Carpenter's men had abandoned him for higher wages on the Virginia Central Railroad, but those who stayed had

Greenwood Depot and Tunnel, 1916. *Center left*: a mail pickup crane. *Courtesy of the C&O.*

finished laying tracks to the perilous Greenwood Tunnel. The chief engineer was pleased to tell the board, "I do not feel any longer any apprehension of danger under the awful impending mass as the eastern portal, whose enormous pressure had actually crushed timbers one foot square. That this dangerous work has been brought to a successful completion without the least accident reflects much credit on the contractor Mr. John Kelly." The date inscribed on a granite plaque for the east portal may refer to the year of boring through, not completion of the passage: "C. Crozet, Chief Engineer, E.T.D. Meyers, Resident Engineer, John Kelly, Contractor, A.D. 1852."[143]

One and a half miles of roadbed west of the Greenwood Tunnel were ready for tracks, but progress stopped for a while on the eighty-foot embankment at Dove Spring Hollow—a section that one observer called "fearful looking." Laborers at Dove Spring, knowing they could walk off the job and work for the Virginia Central at any time, demanded, and soon received, a raise. Crozet then instructed Kelly that he should push forward at Dove Spring Hollow with "all possible diligence" for the coming temporary track.[144]

Farther west, John Kelly suspended arching at the Brooksville Tunnel due to inferior bricks, but between Brooksville and Robertson's Hollow, the

The second Brooksville Tunnel was built fifty feet north of the old one at Dove Spring Hollow in 1928. *Courtesy of the C&O Historical Society.*

roadbed was ready for tracks. Progress was slow yet steady at Robertson's Hollow, the little tunnel and Goodloe's Hollow. On the last two miles before the Blue Ridge Tunnel, Crozet reported, "No work of importance remains to be done, and the track could have been laid long ago if it could have been of any service." Beyond the mountain, three spans for the iron bridge over the South River passed Crozet's deflection test and were on their way from Tredegar Iron Works in Richmond.[145]

The only good news at the Blue Ridge Tunnel was William Crouse's ventilation machine. "A constant supply of fresh air is afforded to the hands, at the distance of 1300 feet by the work of one mule," Crozet stated, "though the distance begins to be a little too much for his strength." As the tunnel lengthened, the addition of a strong horse would clear smoky air, he wrote, "speedily after blasts."[146]

Otherwise, Crozet had nothing positive to say about the main tunnel. He had anticipated 960 feet of excavation in 1853, but the men excavated only 725 feet because they encountered several veins of water amounting to a "sort of a trough," as Crozet described it. The cache produced more than six thousand gallons of water every hour. Then a mass of roof on the west side collapsed on three headers. They were not "materially injured," Crozet wrote, though the payroll stated they were disabled. In a subsequent letter, Crozet reported that the accident "came very near costing the life of two men."[147]

After the roof cave-in, Crozet ordered immediate timbering, but the men were leery and refused to enter the tunnel. Unpredictable rock, combined with the labor scarcity and shortened deadlines, threatened a massive failure of the Blue Ridge Railroad and, as a consequence, a route to the Ohio River. In Crozet's mind, only slave labor could save the project now. The chief engineer had been in contact with local slaveholders since August, keeping the board informed of his efforts. He broached the subject again at the end of his November 1853 letter to Richmond: "Lastly, gentlemen, as the hiring season [for slaves] is close at hand, we can without difficulty secure permanent and reliable labor for next year, which will do away with the fluctuations which have considerably retarded the progress of last year."[148]

By December 1853, the price of white labor had fallen in other parts of the country. Heartened by the news, Crozet was hopeful that the 1853 raises were the last pay increases on the Blue Ridge Railroad. His final 1853 report to the board presented his ideas for slave labor at the Blue Ridge Tunnel in 1854:

The question presents itself, whether we must continue to carry on the work of the main Tunnel with white hands, as heretofore, or resort to the hiring of a black force, which must be done at this time.

I do not think that we could employ exclusively black labor; nor would it answer to work both kinds in immediate contact; but we might, I believe, hire one hundred negroes, who could be advantageously employed on work distinct from that of the Irish hands, as for instance, in attending to the pumps.[149]

Though no conflict had occurred between Irish and slaves on the Blue Ridge Railroad, Claudius Crozet perceived that it might. And he had seen that the Irish were capable of violence, especially the Corkonians. He had no idea what would happen if slaves joined Irish workers at the Blue Ridge Tunnel in January 1854.

9

A FEARFUL VELOCITY

Claudius Crozet's January 1854 letter to the Board of Public Works was low-spirited. Despite the addition of supporting timbers, rock on the west side of the Blue Ridge Tunnel was streaked with long fissures of wet, red clay and still unstable. He told the board that he witnessed an "enormous fall of large loose rocks" at the end of December 1853. A "more considerable" tumble, he wrote, took place the next day.[150]

As a result, Crozet recommended that the men blast holes not deeper than one foot. He admitted that he was in "constant dread of a serious accident which would, in all probability, irretrievably disperse the hands. Those who are now engaged on this hazardous work are entitled to high credit and I have advanced their pay to $1.50 during the continuance of this danger." Some of the west-side men had already abandoned their jobs for "less exposed situations," Crozet reported. On the east side, an insufficient number of drillers meant that auxiliary laborers such as cart loaders and dumpers could do no work on the tunnel proper. Progress was at a standstill.[151]

Crozet's plan for hired slave labor in the Blue Ridge Tunnel also stalled. Richmond slaveholders, or those who congregated in the city to buy, sell and hire slaves, were already skeptical about safety in the passage. When they heard about the roof cave-ins, they would be even less inclined to lease slave labor. Richmond slave agents George W. Toler and John R. Cook specialized in hiring out slaves. They thought they could scrounge a few men at the high price of $200 a year. Crozet rejected the hires as too costly and inadequate for replacing Irish workers with slaves on each side of the tunnel.

"For drilling & blasting, we must have all negroes, or none," he stated, "that is, we must have at once 120 [slave] hands…or else the number hired would have to mix with the white hands."[152]

William Sclater, Crozet's manager, reported the same reluctance from Albemarle County slaveholders. Only George Farrow was willing to hire out slaves for tunnel labor. He and his brother-in-law, David Hansborough, cannily waited until the last week of December 1853. Then they negotiated an exacting contract for forty slaves to work in the tunnel. The agreement stated that the men could not be employed in loading gunpowder or in blasting. It further stipulated that "in case any of said negroes should be injured by any accident resulting immediately from his employment on the work, the Board of Public Works agrees to pay the damage done to said negro or negroes."[153]

Exploiting the wage increase that the Irish had gained for themselves the previous spring, George Farrow bargained a higher pay rate for the slaves. Instead of a lesser, yearly lump sum, the Blue Ridge Railroad paid him a daily wage of $1.12½ a day for each man's work while blacksmiths earned $1.40 a day for him. The Irish wages were more than Crozet wished, but slaves clearing debris would mean a full force of Irish at the drills. Equally important for Crozet, the Blue Ridge Railroad now had a modicum of backup labor as leverage. This would discourage the "old, inefficient force," as he called the predominately Irish work crews, from walking out with no notice and embarrassing him as they had done in the 1853 strike.[154]

Most of the Farrow slaves would work as floorers, but floorers also died in the Blue Ridge Tunnel—three in the previous year—and the slaves would have known it. "When brought to the tunnel, 10 of them ran away," Crozet complained, "and were withdrawn by their masters: for, at present, in hiring, it appears that negroes have become masters of their masters. Those who remain work well and are satisfied. I hope they will induce others to join them." The wording suggests that the runaways returned to their quarters at Brooksville.[155]

Speed and labor for the coming temporary track were all-important as the New Year turned. Greenwood Tunnel, 538 feet long, was finished by late December 1853 with the assistance of Irish engineer Denis Shanahan. A graduate of the University of Dublin, Shanahan fled the Great Hunger with his mother and siblings in 1849. He eventually ended up at Rockfish Gap, where his talents became obvious to John Kelly and Claudius Crozet. With the easternmost tunnel now in operation, Crozet rushed all of his contractors toward completion of other parts of the state road that

Greenwood Tunnel closed when the C&O Railway blasted a parallel cut and laid new tracks in 1944. *Courtesy of the Library of Congress.*

connected with the Virginia Central temporary road. His first priority was grading the temporary track around Kelly's Cut. The grading would ensue "as soon as the black force returns to work," Crozet wrote. The crew on this section consisted of men whom Crozet's manager, William Sclater, had hired from various Albemarle County slaveholders on January 1, 1854. Their work began on January 9.[156]

Sclater had moved from Fluvanna County to Albemarle in 1850. He found living quarters near the Mechum's River construction and employed the services of Maria Evans, a free cook. She is the only black woman known to be associated with the Blue Ridge Railroad. Now that the Mechum's River depot was open, Sclater had quick train access to slaveholders in much of Albemarle. He "searched the country for some distance," Crozet wrote, but could not find the sixty hired slaves for finalizing tracks that he had promised the chief engineer. The thirty-seven men Sclater did hire served the local economy well.[157]

William Wallace's general store was located below what was known as Kelly's Hollow in Greenwood, Virginia. A page from the store's ledger shows charges for moving Sclater's "servants" up to the mountain in January 1854. Other expenses on Sclater's page for that year related to the slaves' food—pork, beef, milk—and their work, which involved horses or mules. Wages for each slave were $150 per year, plus clothes, a hat and one blanket. How much, if any, of the wages the slaveholders allowed the men to keep is unknown. As their general superintendent, Sclater received $100 a month. He portioned the slaves into two crews working thirteen miles apart. George D. Harris was foreman of the crew at the top of Rockfish Gap. James H. Jarman, owner of three of the slaves, including a boy, was foreman of the crew on the east side in Albemarle County. Jarman was a "most efficient man," according to Crozet.[158]

Claudius Crozet needed efficiency. His long race to the Ohio River was, for now, a shorter competition with Charles Ellet. Crozet was confident that the Blue Ridge Railroad and Virginia Central would finish their respective sections of temporary track at about the same time. Ellet was just as certain that the Virginia Central would finish earlier. Crozet disagreed, telling the board that he was "better acquainted than the Engineer of the Company with the character of this mountain."[159]

More tension developed over materials. For Blue Ridge Railroad sections east of Rockfish Gap, Crozet had ordered an ample supply of spikes, cross ties and chairs—the fasteners that fixed cross ties to the rails. In what he termed "much confusion" over the simultaneous laying of tracks by both railroads, five hundred chairs were unaccounted for. All the kegs of spikes had disappeared, as well. Crozet implied pilfering when he obliquely told the board, "It will be impossible, until the tracks are all laid, to know exactly the quantity that may have been used by both parties."[160]

During a marathon of work in the early months of 1854, laborers finished the little tunnel and finalized tracks and embankments on the east

Remnant of the temporary track around the old Brooksville Tunnel. *Author's collection.*

side of Rockfish Gap. On the west side, they raised the South River Bridge and erected a short-term depot in Staunton. The temporary railroad was ready for its first trial run on March 13. Thirteen and a quarter miles of it were Blue Ridge Railroad tracks. Cars filled with forty to fifty passengers followed a locomotive that had already been hauled over the mountain. The train steamed across the South River and climbed the western slope in fifteen minutes. Then it crested the mountain on a tight, 300-foot curve that barely allowed room for the locomotive. For twenty-five minutes, it descended a steep grade—296 feet per mile at one place—on the east side of Rockfish Gap.[161]

Early on the morning of March 20, a passenger train made the first regular run to Staunton. The sound of a shrill whistle that would "wake snakes," according to the *Vindicator*, startled the town folk. Crowds rushed from their beds to see the "elephant," the *Spectator* reported, adding, "There were not a few who apparently regarded it as a thing of life, approaching it with the utmost caution, and touching its exterior with extreme tenderness."[162]

The temporary track was completed in seven months. Charles Ellet called it the "most remarkable railroad now in use." It was proof, he wrote, that the "modern locomotive with its train may now surmount the Alps themselves." But the overly confident Ellet had a lapse of judgment on March 28. Curious about how well a passenger car would coast down the eastern slope with no power and only partly applied brakes, he disconnected the car from the locomotive just ahead. About thirty people were in the car, including Ellet.[163]

The *Charlottesville Jeffersonian Republican* described the accident that occurred when the brake chain snapped:

> *We began to descend with fearful velocity, and as there was a curve ahead of us, those on the locomotive did not discover us till we were within 20 feet of them, and a crash was inevitable. It was awful to anticipate this crash. In an instant we came together. Those on the engine were swept off onto the road with the house of the engine, and fortunately escaped without injury. Those of us who were in the car were prostrated amid the wreck of the seats.* The Lexington Gazette *reported that a railroad employee was standing on the engine platform. As the passenger car hurtled down toward the rear of the locomotive, he leapt off and fell on the tracks. The wheels of the passenger car passed over one of his arms and both legs, cutting off one above the knee and the other below the knee. He died within a few hours.*[164]

A second calamity followed on April 6. Ordered by a Virginia Central superintendent to bring loads of soil to Staunton, a Virginia Central engine man proceeded up the west side of the mountain with flatcars behind the locomotive, as usual. Slaves on William Sclater's Blue Ridge Railroad crew, including two men named Jerry and Thomas, were waiting near the west portal of the Blue Ridge Tunnel. They loaded the freight cars with soil at 6:00 a.m. and climbed on board for the trip down the mountain. George Harris, the foreman responsible for their safety, was eating breakfast. He failed to notice that the departing train was headed back down the western slope with the flatcars ahead of the locomotive. When the cars hit a curve, they detached from the engine and rolled down the tracks, unchecked. The engine man shouted for the slaves to jump off, but Jerry, Thomas and a third slave hung on. Gaining speed on the steep grade, the cars crossed the South River Bridge at what Claudius Crozet later estimated was thirty miles an hour. A handcar, unseen, was sitting around a curve. The flatcars collided with it, killing Jerry and Thomas.[165]

Train work was contrary to agreements that the Board of Public Works had made for slaves on William Sclater's crew. Those contracts specified only

Remnant of the temporary track, now overgrown with trees, on a man-made embankment at Goodloe Hollow. *Author's collection.*

breaking up rock for ballast, ramming it in and otherwise completing the roadbed. Albemarle County slaveholders James Garland and Andrew M. Woods sought compensation for the loss of Jerry and Thomas. They hired an attorney who wrote to Claudius Crozet:

> *At the suggestions of my friends Mr J Garland, & Woods, the owners of two negro men, recently killed on the state work, under your charge, (and*

said negroes hired I believe through the agency of Mr Sclater, by you, for the Board of Public Works) I address you for the purpose of ascertaining whether any difficultys will be interposed to [press] the Board of P Works making compensation to the Gentlemen above named for their loss of these servants.[166]

Witnesses were then called before an Albemarle County justice of the peace. William Sclater testified he had known Thomas since January 1, 1854. He "was a good working hand about twenty years old," Sclater said, "about six feet high of good appearance excepting a small scar on his temple where he had been burned and as far as I known [*sic*] healthy." Sclater estimated that Thomas was worth $1,200. Another witness certified that Jerry was worth $1,250 and that his "character was remarkably good he was about twenty one years of age, his personal appearance was very fine he being tall and strait, his health was perfectly good."[167]

The issue of which railroad would pay for the slaves' monetary worth reached the state's attorney general. Though the incident involved Virginia Central Railroad employees, he ruled that the Board of Public Works was liable for the cost of the slaves. The state must reimburse a reasonable sum out of money appropriated for the Blue Ridge Railroad. Negative publicity for this and Charles Ellet's disastrous experiment cost Crozet dearly. A series of newspaper articles over the following months so heavily criticized the chief engineer that he pleaded for help. "Most scurrilous and unfair attacks directed against me have appeared in some papers, especially the 'Valley Star,'" he wrote a friend. "I come, therefore, to beg you if any such publication appears again in that paper to send it to me."[168]

Meanwhile, Irish injuries and deaths further reduced Crozet's labor force. A header at the Blue Ridge Tunnel lost his leg; the limb was buried at Thornrose Cemetery in Staunton. Two months later, the man's name disappeared from the Blue Ridge Tunnel payrolls. A fifty-six-year-old crew boss who seldom missed a day of work died of paralysis in June. Exposure to fine silica dust created by explosions left the tunnel workers vulnerable to lung diseases. Pleurisy, pneumonia and tuberculosis claimed six laborers and just as many of their womenfolk and children, all from County Cork, before July 1854. The cholera epidemic at the tunnel that began that month would kill many more.[169]

The *Spectator* and *Vindicator* followed the progress of cholera from Richmond to Staunton between June and September 1854. The texts represented the prevailing attitude in America that the disease struck only black people and potato-eating immigrants. "Who Are Victims to the Cholera?" the

Vindicator asked. "The *New York Journal of Commerce*, in speaking of the cholera patients, says: A considerable proportion for the patients received are those who have been of intemperate habits…In one instance, the other day, a post mortem examination showed the contents of the stomach to be made up of a mixture of pieces of cabbage and cabbage-stalks, beets, large pieces of unmashed potatoes, etc."[170]

The cholera epidemic at Rockfish Gap may have originated from Chesapeake Bay oysters containing the bacteria. Papers in Baltimore, Maryland, reported that people who had eaten raw oysters from the bay were suddenly dying. The *Alexandria Gazette* confirmed that oysters from the bay and its tributaries were "poisonous this season." Chesapeake merchants would have shipped the highly popular mollusk to Richmond, where the first case of cholera struck in June. The *Vindicator* reported that cholera cases in the city were "principally confined to the dissipated in habit and the careless in diet." At its July peak, the Richmond epidemic killed forty-two "colored persons."[171]

Cholera traveled next along the James River and Kanawha Canal to the Scottsville landing in Albemarle County. The disease may have arrived via a Richmond boatman already exposed to it. The first of twenty-five "persons of intemperate habits," as the *Spectator* termed victims, died in Scottsville on June 24. Cholera reached the east side of the Blue Ridge Tunnel in July. It was carried, perhaps, by infected draymen who hauled supplies for the Blue Ridge Tunnel from Scottsville up to the tunnel area in Nelson County.[172]

Panic and flight were typical reactions to cholera on public works in the nineteenth century. While working at the Chesapeake and Ohio Canal in 1832, one engineer wrote, "In some instances when the disease has attacked them the invalid has been enticed from the shandee [*sic*] & left to die under the shade of some tree." Such may have been the case with Thomas Mahoney (also Mahaney), a thirty-year-old header at the Blue Ridge Tunnel who went missing in mid-July. Possibly the first victim of the disease at the tunnel, Mahoney's body was not found for two weeks; Augusta County death records noted his date of death as July 17. The cause was "cramp cholic," one of many terms used for cholera at the time.[173]

Murder, either by fellow workers or frightened local citizens, also occurred during cholera epidemics on public works. At Duffy's Cut on the Pennsylvania Railroad, historical records and forensic evidence show that members of an Irish railroad crew suffered from cholera in 1832. Blunt-force trauma is indicated on the skulls of two of the fifty-seven immigrants, including a woman, while a third skull has a possible bullet hole. When rumors of violence spread about

A Celtic cross commemorating the deaths of fifty-seven Irish railroad laborers at Duffy's Cut, Pennsylvania, in 1832. *From Wikipedia Commons.*

Thomas Mahoney, Claudius Crozet intervened with an amateur diagnosis meant to forestall a mass exodus from the Blue Ridge Tunnel shanties. His letter about the epidemic to the *Charlottesville Jeffersonian Republican* stated:

> *I will take this opportunity to correct another report published in some papers, that a man who had been missing, was found recently in a ravine with marks of violence. This man disappeared some two weeks ago; search was made for him, but it was only recently that his body was discovered, <u>without any marks of violence</u>—he had been seen going along the work of a very hot day, and it is probable he was sun struck, sought the shade and died—he was a sober inoffensive man.* [174]

While Thomas Mahoney's body moldered in the ravine, cholera began to ravage the occupants of eight shanties on the east side of the Blue Ridge Tunnel. Then, while Father Daniel Downey nursed the sick and dying, the disease spread to the west side. [175] The *Vindicator* reported:

> *We learn from a private letter, that the cholera still exists at the Tunnel, and fears are entertained that it is extending. Up to Sunday last there had been 20 deaths. It has extended to other localities at the Eastern end of the Tunnel, than the few shanties to which it has hitherto been confined. It has also made its appearance on the Western side of the mountain. Two cases occurred on Sunday, both of which have probably terminated fatally before this. Our informant states that there is great consternation among the Irish laborers.* [176]

At least thirty-three Irish died of cholera during the 1854 epidemic. Thornrose Cemetery in Staunton was the usual place of interment for Irish Catholic workers because Father Downey could say a full funeral Mass at Saint Francis of Assisi Church and graveside prayers at nearby Thornrose. The Thornrose directors, who decided that no persons of notoriety could be buried there, may have experienced a panic of their own. Fifteen Irish cholera victims were buried with no visible marker at Thornrose. Burial places for the remaining eighteen have never been found. [177]

When the cholera epidemic was completely over in October 1854, Claudius Crozet could turn his attention back to the Blue Ridge Railroad, where John Kelly's modest beginnings as a flour mill worker in County Cork gave him a special rapport with his laborers. "I must do justice to his unflinching energy, skill and perfect control over his men, who expose themselves, even recklessly, wherever he directs them," Crozet wrote the Board of Public Works in November. "Where they are now at work no craven would venture; but his commands are unhesitatingly obeyed; and all the difficulty I experience is rather to impress him and them with the necessity of caution."[178]

Of the Blue Ridge Tunnel, Crozet could report nothing new, except that arching on the dangerous center section was a delicate operation and he worried about "incautious blasting." Labor in the passage for the coming year of 1855 was of more concern. George Farrow's contract for the Brooksville slaves would soon expire, and the Christmas hiring season for slaves was fast approaching.[179]

William Sclater composed an offer for an additional fifty to one hundred slaves at the Blue Ridge Tunnel. Emboldened by George Farrow's agreement with the Board of Public Works, Sclater based his proposal on the same terms: the men must work for Irish wages, he insisted, and the board must insure them "against all accidents whatsoever." Sclater was aware that Farrow's foreman had removed the hired slaves from the Blue Ridge Tunnel area for two weeks during the cholera epidemic and that they were unpaid for the lost time. Sclater added a requirement to his proposal: "If there should be any sickness among the hands at the tunnel so that it would not be prudent for the hands to work there they are to be employed somewhere else on the Blue Ridge R Road."[180]

Claudius Crozet enclosed Sclater's proposal in his November 1854 letter to the board. "The white labor is occasionally troublesome," Crozet wrote in support of the offer, "yet, while it continues scarce, we cannot dismiss as freely as proper discipline might require: Black labor would obviate this difficulty."[181]

Crozet need not have worried. The labor situation changed dramatically within the month. As of December 1854, fifty-two new Irish laborers were working in the Blue Ridge Tunnel. Some had returned after a long absence. Perhaps they were previously employed on the Virginia Central Railroad temporary tracks and now in need of a job. Seven of the new hires were youths who had grown old enough for work in the passage. Other newly arrived men were chain migrants from Ireland whose relatives working at the tunnel had sent them passage money. "As regards labor," Crozet informed the Board of Public Works in early December, "things are now very different from what they have been for two years past and we can get hands very readily."[182]

Still, John Kelly and John Larguey had seen in 1854 what slave labor could achieve in the tunnel. They agreed with Crozet that slaves would be an advantage in 1855. The Irishmen understood, as well, their native country's religious customs and the work absences that they created. The Catholic Church designated thirty-two holy days of obligation in the mid-nineteenth century. These honored various saints and celebrated liturgical events such as Easter and Christmas. Attendance at Mass was mandatory. "The numerous holy days of the Irish and their practice to stop work when any one, even a mere child, dies, causes a considerable loss of time," Crozet complained to the Board of Public Works. "This was severely felt during the sickly year just elapsed; when, frequently, for every death, there was a suspension of labor sometimes of two days, which, here, not only occasions delay, but likewise adds to the cost of the work."[183]

As the Christmas hiring season grew ever nearer in early December, Crozet again emphasized slave labor. He was hoping that the arrival of more Irish workers would result in lower Irish wages and, by default, lower slave wages. "If the Board will again hire negroes," he wrote, "the safest plan would be to do so upon some sliding scale regulated by the price of white labor."[184]

Crozet must have sensed that the Irish, already subdued by cholera and competing slave labor in the tunnel in 1854, felt powerless in the face of more slave labor in 1855. At the end of December 1854, the chief engineer dropped wages down to 1853 pre-strike levels with no apparent opposition. "Gentlemen," he wrote the board, "I have the honor to report, that the recent facility of obtaining white hands, has enabled us to reduce the price of labour in both tunnels to one dollar, which is as low a rate as the lowest price at which we were offered negroes.[185]

"In consequence of this favorable change," Crozet continued, "and seeing that, at your last meeting, you inclined to the opinion not to employ negroes, I concluded that, under present circumstances, it was not advisable to mix again white and black labor in the tunnel."[186]

It is unclear why Crozet and the Board of Public Works changed their minds about slave labor. Board members may have wanted to avoid paying insurance or compensation for the loss of slaves, as they had for Jerry and Thomas. Or the board's decision might have come from a floating fear, shared by Crozet, that the Irish would blame the slaves for their drop in wages and retaliate by attacking them. It is also unclear why the Irish passively accepted a painful pay cut when working conditions at the Brooksville and Blue Ridge Tunnels were so unsafe. Crozet had lobbied for the use of more slave labor, lowered Irish wages and then did not use slave labor after all. The Irish should have lost patience with his sleight of hand. But winter had arrived, and six Blue Ridge Tunnel workers and family members died in December. The sorrowful events of 1854 may have left the people too exhausted for protest.

APPALLING DIFFICULTIES

By 1855, dangers in the Brooksville Tunnel seemed insurmountable. Only 184 feet were left to blast in the 868-foot-long passage. Yet the difficulties were "so appalling," Crozet told the Board of Public Works, that he considered abandoning the tunnel and replacing it with an open cut. He soon decided that this option was too costly. At the west heading, 60 feet in from the west portal, the pressure of the mountain crushed wooden arches. The damage left a "confused mass of rocks, clay, and broken timbers," Crozet wrote. The fall of rocks and loose earth from an unknown height in the chasm above was so frequent that replacing the timbers was nearly impossible. At the east heading, 150 feet in from the east portal, workers found the same treacherous conditions. Fortunately, well-made bricks arching the east portal withstood rock falls that exerted a pressure of 2,400 pounds per square inch. But earth slides at both openings required repeated removal after heavy rain. Slides happened so often that Brooksville Tunnel payrolls had separate "bank and slides" lists for the men, boys and horses who shored up the damage. The remaining laborers braved work inside the passage.[187]

Dangers also continued at the Blue Ridge Tunnel. On January 29, 1855, three men on the east side were "dreadfully wounded and mangled," according to the *Richmond Daily Dispatch*, while removing a charge that failed to explode. One of them died within a few days. Though Claudius Crozet omitted the accident in his letters to the board, it surely spurred the strike that took place two months later.[188]

John Kelly's leadership qualities at the Brooksville and Blue Ridge Tunnels were becoming well known in Richmond's halls of power. "At times the work has been accompanied by such threatening aspects," the Board of Public Works reported to the general assembly, "that the laborers have retreated from it in dismay, and under a less intrepid and indomitable contractor, they could hardly have been persuaded to return."[189]

Had John Kelly's men abandoned their perilous work, the railroad might have found willing replacements eventually; the labor shortage on the Blue Ridge Railroad eased in 1855 as more Irish immigrants poured into the country. But it is doubtful that any other contractor on the project would have saved the entire venture with his own money. In early 1855, a financial crisis crippled the state government. When bonds fell below their stated value, the board was unable to pay Kelly and Company for work at both unfinished tunnels. Nor could it pay for the embankment still under construction east of the Blue Ridge Tunnel. Beginning in March 1855, Kelly and John Larguey bought all supplies out of pocket. They also paid the laborers' wages. Yet this was not an ideal situation for the state because Crozet wanted to lower pay yet again.[190] He informed the board:

> *While these circumstances may be the occasion of congratulation that we have so far succeeded with the means advanced by the contractor, it is desirable that this arrangement should not continue much longer. While credit is due him for his energy and perseverance, it is obvious that it keeps the work to a certain extent in a state of dependence. So long, for example, as the hands are retained chiefly by their confidence in the contractor and do not receive their full pay, it must be difficult to obtain a further reduction of their wages, which might otherwise be attempted.*[191]

Crozet's plan for reducing pay failed when Irish at the Blue Ridge Tunnel went on strike again in March 1855. "We are trying to ferret out the ringleaders," Crozet informed the board. "I regret that we did not hire Negroes at Christmas." The strike was a partial success. Some, though not all, headers and floorers received their post-1853 strike pay of $1.25 a day. Boys' wages rose to $1.00 a day—their highest yet. Crozet paid for the increases by dropping the pay of teamsters and some blacksmiths. Three of the smiths were Brooksville slaves who continued working at the Blue Ridge Tunnel after 1854.[192]

Apparently the pay raise motivated the Irish to increase their work pace. Though drill bits often dulled before piercing the rock—sometimes forty drills were used to bore one hole—the men averaged about 2.5 feet a day from both sides. Slowly they crept toward perforation of the Blue Ridge Tunnel in the spring and summer of 1855. By August, 952 feet remained. Crozet predicted the men would bore through late in the following year. Elsewhere on the railroad, the embankment at Robertson's Hollow was now 80 feet high and up to the desired grade. Slaves on William Sclater's crew completed almost all of the ballasting for sections of track not yet controlled by the Virginia Central. Those roadbeds were now ready for tracklayers.[193]

The possibility of a second cholera outbreak threatened progress at the Blue Ridge Tunnel when one-year-old Eugene Quinn died on August 4. Eugene was the youngest son of Hannah and John Quinn, an Irish mason of master status who worked on all four of the Blue Ridge Railroad tunnels. The child was buried with a plain fieldstone marker in the graveyard—now known as the Quinn Cemetery—at the back of George Farrow's property. Eugene and his mother were likely the subject of a *Charlottesville Advocate* article on August 5, which stated that a child at the tunnel had died of cholera the previous day. "The cause of the cholera," the paper noted, "is properly attributed to the spoilt meat, and large quantities of coarse vegetables these hands consume, and to their excessive filthiness."[194]

Claudius Crozet again intervened with an untrained diagnosis of sunstroke in a letter that he wrote to the *Richmond Daily Dispatch*. The paper reported:

> *We published a day or two since, a report from the Charlottesville* Advocate *to the effect that there had been one fatal case of cholera at Blue Ridge Tunnel, and one so near fatal that the patient, a woman, was shrouded ready for burial. Col. Crozet, engineer of the Tunnel, contradicts the report, and says that the fatal case was that of an infant, who died of cholera morbus, and the case of the woman who was shrouded for burial and revived, was the result of a sun stroke. The Tunnel was never more healthy at the same season than it is now.*[195]

Cholera morbus is now identified as gastroenteritis. Sometimes infectious, it was often confused with the cholera bacteria, *Vibrio cholera*, by nineteenth-century doctors. Either might have caused Hannah Quinn's illness and her son's death.

By year's end, Claudius Crozet was appreciative of men such as John Quinn who had labored, with deep personal loss, for half a decade on the Blue Ridge Railroad. When the board pressed for a workforce reduction, the chief engineer asked them to reconsider. "After having experienced great

A rubbing of the footstone for Eugene and Mary Quinn. Eugene's sister, Mary, died on August 4, 1856, exactly one year after his death. *Author's collection.*

difficulty, for a long time in procuring an adequate complement of hands," he wrote, "we have at last secured not only a sufficient force, but also a number of chosen, experienced men, on whom we can depend, and who are well settled on the work, most of them with families; but who, if suffered to leave, could not be again collected for the short period requisite to complete it."[196]

Crozet admitted that retaining a full complement of men would be a financial sacrifice, but it was the only practical way to complete the Blue Ridge Railroad. Finding enough money to maintain the workforce was just one of many problems on Virginia's public works during the 1855 financial crisis. The $1 million that the state had appropriated for construction of the Covington and Ohio Railroad was also running out. Contractors would soon be left with no funds for the grading they had begun west of Covington.[197]

With the state budget so constrained, even the cost of blasting powder was a concern. In 1851, the price of one hundred kegs was $227. By October 1855, it was almost double that amount. When writing to the board about the "extraordinary rise" of the cost of gunpowder and other commodities, Crozet estimated the price of finishing the Blue Ridge Railroad at $140,000.[198]

The Blue Ridge Railroad consumed almost 1,300 kegs of gunpowder in 1856. Most of it was used in the Blue Ridge Tunnel, where a second Dan Sullivan from County Cork died in a blast in March that year. By June, six tunnel workers and eight women and children in the shanties were dead from pneumonia, tuberculosis and other causes. Losing heart, some of the Irish laborers migrated north in search of better wages. Those on the west side of the mountain with the tenacity to keep working threatened a strike that partly succeeded. Carpenters and blacksmiths received a pay increase. Wages for floorers—who, by far, represented the largest number of men employed at the Blue Ridge Tunnel—stayed the same. Experienced headers and blasters saw their pay rise to $1.37½ a day.[199]

Completion of the Blue Ridge Railroad was now a matter of feet instead of miles, and the Virginia Central's Covington extension needed only one and one-half miles of heavy labor at Millboro in Bath County—where hundreds of Irish were working on the line—and ten miles of track east of Covington in Alleghany County. The Covington and Ohio Railroad, however, still lacked additional state funding by 1856. Directors of the Virginia Central saw no reason to finish the Covington extension until the railroad from the west was complete. The directors deferred all construction contracts in April 1856, stating that "they shall remain suspended until there is a prospect of having a portion of the Covington and Ohio opened for use."[200]

None of the delays stopped a group of Richmond and Staunton dignitaries from touring completed sections of the railroad at the height of a drought in July 1856. Charles Ellet was one of the passengers. "We rushed along rapidly and merrily," wrote an accompanying newspaper reporter from Richmond. The men stopped for a meal at Mechum's River Hotel. Then, with "slow irresistible power," the locomotives climbed Rockfish Gap on the temporary rails. The track was an achievement, the reporter enthused, "which ought to immortalize Mr. Ellet."[201]

The passenger cars were crowded with travelers to Virginia's famed natural springs, though a few miles by stagecoach at the end of the line were still necessary. Resorts were a significant source of revenue for the Virginia Central. In one week alone that dry summer of 1856, seven hundred visitors journeyed to the Greenbrier resort at White Sulphur Springs and five hundred to Rockbridge Alum Springs. These were only two of many watering places, as they were called, that profited when east Virginians sought cooler mountain temperatures. The men finished their tour with a banquet at the Millboro Spring. "The party broke up in high spirits," the reporter concluded, "all wishing that the people of the State could only see for themselves what they had seen that day, for surely there would be but one voice in Virginia towards the Central Railroad, and that would be 'GO AHEAD.'"[202]

On the Blue Ridge Railroad, workers did go ahead. A skeleton crew of nineteen men and one horse finished Brooksville Tunnel in October 1856, though workers continued to stabilize the steep Dove Spring Hollow area for another year. Crozet assured the Board of Public Works that the strength of the three-foot-thick brick arch in the tunnel was "tested by immense masses of rock, which have fallen upon it from a height not less than one hundred feet." Generous again with his praise for John Kelly, Crozet noted that the contractor's "personal exposure, constant attendance and confidence kept hands at work, who more than once manifest a disposition to quit; and this under well-known circumstances of financial difficulties, which, but for him, would inevitably have stopped the work."[203]

At the Blue Ridge Tunnel, Crozet could report by October 1856 that the "drills from one side to the other are now heard very plainly." That same month, the Virginia Central Railroad heralded the success of the temporary track over Rockfish Gap. Giving Claudius Crozet no credit for his part in the project, and evading the loss of life on early runs, Virginia Central directors reported to stockholders that the "perfect success with which the mountain track has been operated for two years, without the slightest accident since it was regularly opened for public use, is…of justifiable pride with our engineer, Mr. Ellet, under whose direction it was constructed."[204]

Charles Ellet was a man of many engineering talents, but he had never designed a tunnel. Aware that the boring through of the Blue Ridge Tunnel would soon overshadow his most recent accomplishment at the temporary track, he published a history of the project in early December 1856. He avoided direct mention of Claudius Crozet and John Kelly. Instead he wrote that the mountaintop track was constructed in "opposition to considerable professional and official resistance."[205]

On Sunday, December 28, Crozet sent one of his former assistant engineers a telegram, asking him to join him the following day when the "headings of the tunnel would meet." Fifty-two men and eight boys were laboring on both sides of the Blue Ridge Tunnel on December 29. Witnesses

Blue Ridge Tunnel west portal, 1937. The photographer, James Brumfield, grew up in nearby Waynesboro, Virginia, and often visited the passage. *Courtesy of Dale Brumfield.*

on the east side included Crozet and his former assistant engineer, John Kelly; engineer Denis Shanahan, who now assisted Kelly at the Blue Ridge Tunnel; and James Alexander of the *Charlotttesville Jeffersonian Republican*. Presumably John Larguey was on the west side, standing by as a driller ground away the final inches of rock.[206]

Three days later, the *Richmond Daily Dispatch* described the event:

> *On Monday morning the augurs met and the perforation was achieved. They were not more than half an inch apart. The Irish laborers were delighted on the occasion, and struck work, swearing they would do no more until next year: i.e., 1857…So accurately had been all the calculations made by Col. Crozet, that the auger holes from both ends of the Tunnel were only half an inch distant from each other, when they met, and the difference in the length of the tunnel as computed by measurement on the outside, over the top of the mountain, and as accurately measured inside, after the perforation, was less than six inches…Several toasts, pertinent to the occasion, were drank in whiskey and cold water.*[207]

PEAKS AND HOLLOWS

Perforation of the Blue Ridge Tunnel was a thrilling milestone, but it only heightened public eagerness for a permanent railroad. The need for trains became even more apparent when a snowstorm disabled the temporary track for ten days in January 1857. Staunton publisher Joseph Waddell remembered that "as there was then no telegraph line to Staunton, the people of the town and the county were cut off from communication with the outside world…At 4 o'clock Wednesday, January 28th, the first train from Richmond arrived with thirty bags of mail for the Staunton post office."[208]

One of those mailbags would have held a copy of the January 28 edition of the *Richmond Daily Dispatch*, delivered to Joseph Waddell. The paper led with a front-page, multicolumn account of the Blue Ridge Railroad and its four tunnels. The article observed that the Blue Ridge Tunnel passed under one of the highest peaks at Rockfish Gap, whereas both portals were in hollows. Addressing the recurrent criticism of Crozet, the paper stated, "It is owing to this fact that the use of shafts has not been resorted to, a very simple calculation showing that while these would have been enormously expensive, they would scarcely have accelerated the perforation."[209]

The article further described the stone arch at the west portal as a "handsome and massive piece of masonry." A six-foot by seven-foot inscribed marble slab was inserted at the top of the arch. John Kelly and John Larguey had stepped forward to finance construction of the very tunnel on which the plaque hung. The absence of their names on the slab was an unfortunate omission.

This Work was constructed by the Commonwealth of Virginia
It was commenced in 1850
Under the direction of the Board of Public Works
President
Jno. B. Floyd, Governor.
Directors
Robert Butler, Treasurer.
Robert Johnston, 1ˢᵗ Auditor
Claudius Crozet, Chief Engineer.
Jas. Brown, Jr. 2ⁿᵈ Auditor
Stafford H. Parker, Register Land Office.
A.M. Dupuy, Res't Engineer.[210]

Though Kelly and Company was ignored on the plaque, University of Virginia geology students took note of Irish laborers when they toured the Blue Ridge Tunnel in January 1857. One student reported seeing about two hundred workers and a total population of seven hundred, including "men, women, children, and dogs." Those laborers continued to blast away rock and remove debris. Three men died at the tunnel in 1857—one in an accident, another from an isolated incident of cholera and the third of pneumonia. By demand or through Claudius Crozet's largesse, floorers, headers, blasters, crew bosses and masons received a pay raise that year, with some floorers earning a record high of $1.87½ a day. In March, Crozet optimistically predicted that the first train would run through in July. "This is glorious news!" the *Lexington Gazette* declared. "The business of the company will be much increased, the expenses reduced, the public convenience enhanced, and one of the greatest works upon which Virginia ever entered, triumphantly completed."[211]

In the summer of 1857, work crews stabilized slides at Kelly's Cut, and the anticipated July completion of the Blue Ridge Tunnel arrived. Crozet was staying at Brooksville, as usual. Residents at the inn now included Denis Shanahan and his wife, Anne. Shanahan was still employed as assistant engineer at the Blue Ridge Tunnel, but he and Crozet could do little without sufficient laborers. The reduction of headers and floorers that Crozet had opposed forced him to issue another postponement from Brooksville: the Blue Ridge Tunnel would not be finished for six months.[212]

Local newspapers turned vicious. "It will be recollected with what a flourishing of trumpets a few…assembled…to see the hole made through the mountain," the author of a *Charlottesville Advocate* article sniped. "Well that was done in gallant style, and all hands got drunk from the joy at the

Drill holes at the approach to the Blue Ridge Tunnel west portal. *Author's collection.*

prospect of completing the tunnel…It now turns out that Col. Crozet finds it necessary to have the tunnel arched over with brick."[213]

Later in July, the board announced that the Blue Ridge Railroad Company would finish grading the floor of the tunnel. Then, the board stated, the Virginia Central Railroad could assume "management of the arching, etc. under their own engineers." For once, work proceeded according to schedule. The tunnel floor was graded and laid with tracks by September 12, 1857, "somewhat sooner than I had expected," Crozet wrote. Kelly and Company paid final bills for construction expenses and closed their ledger book that same month.[214]

In late September, H.D. Whitcomb, Ellet's replacement as chief engineer for the Virginia Central Railroad, made a cursory examination of the Blue Ridge Tunnel. He determined it was "perfectly safe," though he cautioned that "it may be necessary to arch a portion of the tunnel now unprotected to provide against disintegration, and if so, it should be done at once. I presume that the distinguished gentleman now in charge, and who is perfectly familiar with the roof, will indicate any portions of which there is any doubt. I think we may run through the tunnel in about two weeks."[215]

West portal of the Blue Ridge Tunnel. *Author's collection.*

Still, a permanent railroad was out of the question for now. H.D. Whitcomb anticipated that a "considerable mass of rock" at Kelly's Cut, while stable for the time being, would slide down during the coming winter of 1857–58. Before a permanent track could be laid, thirty to forty men working for six weeks were needed to remove the rock. Moving west in his report, Whitcomb noted similar slides at Dove Spring Hollow, Robertson's Hollow and the steep embankment leading to the Blue Ridge Tunnel's east portal. Here, the only remedy was "supplying material from the top as fast as it slides away below." Whitcomb advised the Virginia Central directors that "slides should be taken notice of in the settlement between you and the Board of Public Works."[216]

Heeding Whitcomb's advice, the Virginia Central Directors resolved, "It is distinctly understood that whatever work may be deemed necessary…should be done at the expense of the state."[217] After a Richmond paper published the resolution, criticism in the *Lexington Gazette* reached a poisonous level:

It now turns out by actual experiment that the Blue Ridge Tunnel is too small to admit the passage of a single car, much less a full train! And it is variously estimated that it will take from three to eighteen months before the defect can be remedied! We do not think that there is another engineer in the State who could have succeeded in the way Col. Crozet has, for almost any man, after an eight year tug, would have been stupid enough to have made the hole big enough for the purpose for which it was designed.[218]

The car in question was a test vehicle. The *American Railroad Journal* reprinted Crozet's response:

The tunnel is elliptical, and closes in towards the top. It is not quite as easy to cut out a regular ellipse through veins of the hardest rock, as to whittle a pine stick; there is always some trimming of projecting points to do in the end. It is not possible to detect, with certainty, the jutting points in the way until a track is laid. Accordingly, as soon as this was done, I caused a frame of the full size of the largest Central railroad cars to be made, 10 feet wide and 11½ high, and moved it along the track. In a few places its upper corner touched, as we set about removing these points. One-half of this small job is already done. On the level of the track, there is ample room for one car and persons to stand on the side while it passes.[219]

Now sixty-eight years old, Claudius Crozet was exhausted by journalistic venom. Late in 1857, he composed his final annual report to the Board of Public Works. Dated January 1, 1858, and the length of a pamphlet, it listed in detail the problems he faced during construction of the Blue Ridge Railroad. The primary impediments, he recounted, were cholera, a shortage of state funds, labor costs and engineering obstacles. "I will retire from your service with a deep sense of gratitude for the flattering confidence which has sustained me through the many trials I have been subject to," he wrote. "It has been my constant study to discharge my duty to the state faithfully. Your countenance satisfies me that I have done so."[220]

The polite formality of Crozet's resignation contrasted sharply with his private letter to the secretary of the board two weeks later. "I think it might have been better for me to continue my supervision of the work," Crozet confessed, "but it will not suffer in proportion as much as I did, to be, notwithstanding my exclusive attention to the State's interest, constantly harassed by the most unfair and insulting misrepresentations…To do everything for the best interest of others, and be rewarded and treated thus! And that by the very people whom I studied to benefit!"[221]

The people had already benefited from Claudius Crozet's engineering vision. Though the Blue Ridge Tunnel was still under construction, busy freight and passenger traffic on the temporary track had created a boom economy in Augusta County. A resident there wrote the *New York Herald*, announcing that employment was available in the area. His call for workers included "farm hands, gardeners, nursery men, blacksmiths, miners, and indeed, common laborers and artisans of every kind. Last year I could not employ laborers on my farm at $51 a month, I boarding them. Good blacksmiths can get from $8–10 a week."[222]

Augusta's prosperity would have been irrelevant to Claudius Crozet by this time. In January 1858, he was living in Georgetown and employed as an engineer on the Washington, D.C. aqueduct. Noting Denis Shanahan's "efficient and intelligent service," he assigned the Irish engineer the task of disposing of Blue Ridge Railroad equipment and supplies. Crozet's replacement was Charles B. Fisk, who, according to Crozet, was "in every way qualified to judge and inspire confidence."[223]

Charles Fisk toured the line in February 1858. He observed that the Blue Ridge Tunnel was probably wide enough for safety but suggested widening the un-arched sections just in case. He also recommended a broader base for embankments at the Blue Ridge Tunnel east portal and at Robertson's Hollow; level steps formed of rocky material at the bottom of the banks would absorb the downward weight of slides. A narrow place at Kelly's Cut needed widening, as well. Otherwise, it was satisfactory. Fisk concluded that the state should pay the Virginia Central Railroad $10,000 for these repairs.[224]

Finally, all was at the ready. A crew of sixty-one men finished up work at the Blue Ridge Tunnel and the east-side embankment on Saturday, April 10, 1858. On the night of April 12, the last train using the temporary track chugged over Rockfish Gap, heading west. On the morning of April 13, a mail train steamed through the Blue Ridge Tunnel, heading east and on time. Five days later, the first passenger train entered the east portal. Newspaperman James Alexander described the experience:

> *On the train approaching either side of it* [the tunnel] *the cars are lighted up and a red light placed on the end of the rear car, the speed is diminished, and every precaution used to prevent accidents. The entire distance can be seen through from the front or rear. The light on the outside of the tunnel assumes, as the cars progress through it, an appearance of a luminous fire, and at last a perfect brilliant blaze.*[225]

Locomotive at Kelly's Cut, circa 1910. *Author's collection.*

The Blue Ridge Tunnel was 4,273 feet long, or four-fifths of a mile. It exceeded the length of the Baltimore and Ohio Railroad's Kingwood and Board Tree Tunnels, which were completed, respectively, in 1852 and 1853. At its broadest point 4 feet above the rails, the egg-shaped passage was between 15 and 18 feet wide. The space was more than sufficient for a Virginia Central Railroad car, which was 9.5 feet wide—exactly 1 foot narrower than a present-day Amtrak passenger car.[226]

The final cost of the tunnel when the state turned it over to the Virginia Central in 1858 was $488,000, but the passage by no means was finished. Irish laborers now employed by the Virginia Central were still knocking or blasting away rocky protrusions and lining the passage with bricks; two men died in the tunnel in April and June 1859.[227]

Later that year, Aquila Johnson Peyton, a twenty-two-year-old schoolteacher, observed the work when she visited the Blue Ridge Tunnel. According to her diary:

We approached the eastern mouth on a high embankment composed entirely of fragments of flinty stone blasted out of the tunnel…Far before us we could see the lights of the blasters, and hear the roar of the hand-cars. When we got up to the stage, our ears were saluted by the sharp din and clank of the drills. On each side were several workmen at different heights with small lamps, perforating the walls with drills. A hand car plying between them and a forge further on, carried the drills to the smiths. This forge had a very dismal appearance.[228]

The village of Afton was born when a post office was established one mile east of the Blue Ridge Tunnel in Nelson County in 1859. By August 1860, only one laborer was still employed at the Blue Ridge Tunnel: Irishman Tim Callaghan, who lived, probably in a shanty, with his family near Afton. About forty Irish families settled in Staunton as the construction decade drew to a close. Some of the men continued employment with the Virginia Central as train hands. Single women worked as domestics while married women earned money as washerwomen, seamstresses and proprietors of boardinghouses. These were standard jobs for female Irish immigrants in the nineteenth century, though one resourceful widow eventually started a retail liquor concern.[229]

Thomas and Ann Fallon from County Roscommon took their first steps toward financial security. In 1860, the family owned two buildings in Staunton. By 1885, their grandson, John, would own three pieces of downtown property, including a large market garden and florist business that flourished for decades. A few Irishmen established businesses in Irish Alley near the Staunton depot. Such enterprises could be fragile. Sixty-year-old John O'Hare, who had lived in an Albemarle County barracks that housed ninety-nine Irish railroad workers in 1850, saved enough from his salary to establish a warehouse on Irish Alley. Then a flood swept through the narrow

Afton Depot, 1949. *Courtesy of the C&O Historical Society.*

street in August 1860. "Irish Alley was completely cleaned of the rubbish which had accumulated there since the last flood," the *Spectator* reported. "The loss is not heavy, but falls on those poorly able to bear it—The floors of the row of store rooms on the wharf gave way as did a part of the foundations. Jno. O'Hare's loss is considerable in goods and damage to the building."[230]

Other Irish veterans of the Blue Ridge Railroad followed construction west. The state allotted more money to the Covington and Ohio Railroad in 1858, hiring contractors of "character, respectability, and long experience." One of them was John Kelly. He moved with his family to the far reaches of Alleghany County, where his men began work on the 460-foot-long Kelly's Tunnel. It was one of eight passages under construction west of Covington in Virginia's push toward the Alleghany Summit. The first of these was Johnson Tunnel—never completed—followed by the Mud, Moore, Lake, Kelly, Lewis, Alleghany and White Sulphur Tunnels. Kelly's men and their families resided in a cluster of twenty-six houses in Alleghany. Probably shanties, these were located near Kelly's dwelling on a remote mountain at Backbone, Virginia. The people's willingness to live in a desolate spot much more isolated than Rockfish Gap proved their fealty to the man who had led them through many trials on the Blue Ridge Railroad.[231]

Kelly's Tunnel near Backbone, Virginia, was converted to a double track in 1889. New portals were added in 1932. *Courtesy of the C&O Historical Society.*

Railroad station at Backbone, Virginia, circa 1900. *Courtesy of the C&O Historical Society.*

Millboro Tunnel, Bath County, Virginia. The passage is still in use. *Courtesy of Paul Collinge.*

The Virginia Central Railroad Board of Directors reinstated contracts in 1860 and resumed work on the original, intended path southwest along the spine of the mountains. Irish laborers built a temporary track around the difficult Millboro Tunnel in Bath while work went forward on the next three tunnels east of Covington: Lick Run and Mason in Bath County and Coleman in Alleghany County. By 1860, almost half of Alleghany County's two thousand residents were Irish who lived and worked along the Virginia Central or Covington and Ohio Railroads. A handful of them, including two floorers and a crew boss who had worked in the Blue Ridge Tunnel, enlisted in the Confederate army when the Civil War began in 1861. The gory conflict delayed railroad construction toward the Ohio River for the next five years.[232]

WESTWARD HO!

The Blue Ridge Railroad played two noteworthy, if minor, roles in the Civil War. On April 22, 1861, five days after Virginia delegates voted for secession from the Union, 175 Virginia Military Institute cadets gathered at the depot in Staunton, Virginia. Dressed in flat-topped caps and cropped blue jackets, the uniformed young men bid goodbye to admiring young ladies and then boarded passenger cars. Their former professor and now general, who would be known as Thomas "Stonewall" Jackson, was with them.[233]

The train also pulled flatcars loaded with baggage and cannons. It was bound for Richmond, but the locomotive slid off the tracks in the Blue Ridge Tunnel. This was the only recorded derailment in the history of the passage. Two hours later, the steam engine was back on the tracks. It headed down the eastern slope for a water and wood stop at Mechum's River depot in western Albemarle County—a place as eager for war as the cadets. "Here, as at other points of the line," Jackson wrote his wife during the refueling, "the War spirit is intense. The cars had scarcely stopped here, before a request was made that I would leave a cadet to drill a company."[234]

Stonewall Jackson and his weary regiments were back at Mechum's River the following spring. After a muddy march from the Shenandoah Valley—home for many of the men—over the mountain on May 3, 1862, they made camp in the hills and fields around the depot. Jackson spent the night at the small hotel located a few yards south of the tracks. Three trains stood on the depot's siding and main rails, ready for transporting the foot troops to Richmond. Early the next morning, the soldiers packed themselves in the cars while cavalrymen mounted their horses. But, in a secret maneuver meant to surprise Union general John Fremont, whose twenty-thousand-man force was assembled in the Allegheny Mountains seventy-five miles west of Staunton, Jackson ordered the trains in the opposite direction. The soldiers cheered as the cars started moving west, back through the Blue Ridge Tunnel to the Shenandoah Valley.[235]

Brooksville Tunnel also claimed a small share of attention during the Civil War. Claudius Crozet had been rightly concerned about the strength of bricks

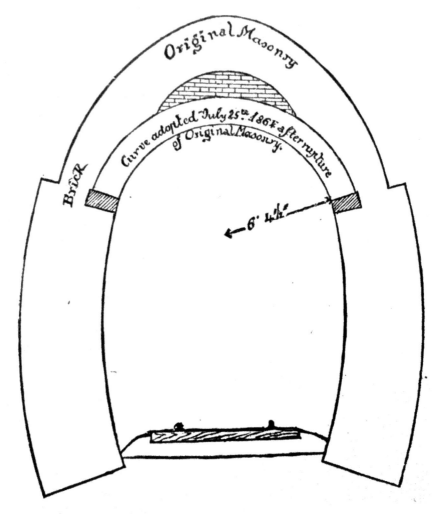

This diagram of Brooksville Tunnel reads: "Brick, Original masonry, Curve adapted July 25th, 1864 after rupture of Original Masonry, 6' 4½.'" *Illustration from* Tunneling, Explosives, and Rock Drills *by Henry Drinker, 1882.*

that arched the passage. By 1863, the mountainside was sliding down on the north side of the tunnel. As the mass of earth pressed on timbers built into the arch, the bricks crumbled. A horizontal crack appeared in the wall, twelve feet above the tunnel floor. "The tunnel was in danger of being closed up," engineer Henry S. Drinker remembered. "It occurred during the civil war, when labor and materials were scarce…A notch was cut in the old wall below the crack 18 inches in depth…the space between the new and old arch was filled with brick and cement, and the timbers which project through the wall removed. Ten feet at a time was as much as could be treated in this manner."[236]

Brooksville slaves whose labor George Farrow had leased for the Blue Ridge Tunnel were experienced and near at hand. They would have been a logical choice to patch up Brooksville Tunnel. Repairs kept it open through the war and beyond, though the entire Virginia Central Railroad line suffered greatly from neglect and Union raids. In 1864, Union forces attacked every station west of Rockfish Gap. They destroyed stone viaducts and the turntable in Staunton, the Staunton depot and the South River Bridge at Waynesboro.[237]

Keeping up with Virginia Central repairs or even normal maintenance was impossible. Mid-war, Edmund Fontaine, president of the Virginia Central, published a request for slaves to mend the tracks. He offered slaveholders forty dollars a month for each man hired. "I need to undertake to enlighten you as to your fate if our Army is compelled to fall back and the enemy takes possession," Fontaine warned. "Will it then be in a source of pleasure to think of the labor you employed in draining your lands, clearing off shrubbery, and dressing up waste places, as many do, in ordinary times, more for ornament than profit?"[238]

The enemy, of course, eventually took possession of Virginia and the Virginia Central Railroad. In Albemarle County, General Philip Sheridan's troops burned the Mechum's River Bridge and the depots at Greenwood, Mechum's River and Woodville (Ivy) in February 1865. Mary Randolph Garrett, a young woman living in Greenwood, Virginia, wrote a letter describing the conflagration. Mary Thomas, Betsey and twenty-five-year-old Monroe were slaves in her household. Garret wrote:

A few moments ago, Mary Thomas heard someone call Betsey and herself, they went out and saw Monroe. They said, why, where are you going, not with the Yankees? Yes, he said, you see me, I am going, and laughed heartily. All Mr Timberlake's men have left and all Mr Farrow's. We have heard that they [Sheridan's troops] *fired on the second train of*

This Civil War photo of a Richmond and Fredericksburg Railroad bridge suggests how Mechum's River Bridge looked after Union troops destroyed it in 1865. *Photographer Tim Sullivan, 1864. Courtesy of the Library of Congress.*

cars that went off [from Greenwood Depot] *yesterday evening. We hear today that the reception room is certainly burnt, as well as the depot room. Some Yankees said they were going to burn the next too* [sic] *depots* [Mechum's River and Woodville] *and then go to Charlottesville and burn the University, and proceed to Lynchburg. A few moments ago we saw the smoke ascending from Meachums river, in black curls…A Yankee told one of the servants that they had a gay time burning the depot. Mr. Bowen's little Ed just came and…says the ticket office was not burnt. Dear. Dear.*[239]

Not all of the Brooksville freedmen left the area. Reuben Ailstock, Thomas Barns, Henry Groves, William Spears and Sandy White—all former laborers at the Blue Ridge Tunnel—chose to live near Brooksville after the war.[240] Flexing his new rights as a citizen, Thomas Barns sued his former slaveholder, David Hansborough—George Farrow's brother-in-law—for back wages due since May 1865. The court ordered Hansborough to pay Barns twenty-four dollars for services rendered on his farm. Presumably Barns never received back pay for his forced work as an enslaved blacksmith at the tunnel.[241]

In September 1865, President Andrew Johnson signed a full pardon and amnesty for George Farrow's participation, direct or implied, in the "late rebellion." Farrow died of heart disease at age fifty-six in 1867. He was likely buried in the private family plot behind the Brooksville house, which still stands.[242]

Surrounded by the sound of Union and Confederate guns, Claudius Crozet died of unknown causes at his daughter's house in Goochland County on January 29, 1864. He was buried at Shockoe Hill Cemetery in Richmond and later reinterred at the Virginia Military Institute. His will stipulated, "As regards my servants, Phoebe and Josephine, I desire their situation to remain as at present as long as they live in the Confederacy; but if either or both express a desire of going out of it, after admonishing them of the probable consequences to themselves of taking such a step, they may be allowed to remove, to any place they may choose for their future home." Josephine was in "delicate health," according to Crozet's will, and worth $1,500. Phoebe's health was "very bad." She was valued at $500. It is unknown if the sickly women acted on his offer of freedom, which presumed they could find safe passage to a free state while traveling alone through a war-torn land.[243]

John Kelly remained in Alleghany County with his family and purchased Sweet Chalybeate Springs for $100,000 in 1862. Formerly known as Red Sweet Springs, the resort featured a thirty-room hotel, three natural springs and an octagonal bathhouse. The resort was set on 1,500 acres in a valley eight miles south of Kelly's Tunnel. The contractor raised livestock as he sat out the war, waiting for railroad construction and travel to the region's springs to resume.[244]

During the war, the Virginia Central Railroad's operating expenses, including tolls it owed the state for use of the Blue Ridge Railroad tracks, exceeded its income. By war's end in 1865, net profit for the road was only $7.17 in U.S. currency. However, $100 in gold was left in the treasury. It was enough to begin immediate repairs. The line between Staunton and Mechum's River opened two months after surrender. By the spring of 1866, all depots were rebuilt, and daily service along the entire line was restored.[245]

Reproduction of Edward Beyer's painting of Red Sweet Springs, later Sweet Chalybeate Springs, 1857. *Author's collection.*

Virginia resumed its prewar stretch toward the Ohio in piecemeal fashion. First, the state reincorporated the Covington and Ohio Railroad in 1866. Working in agreement with the new state of West Virginia, the general assembly passed an act to complete the line to the Ohio River. In 1867, the Virginia Central Railroad hired former Virginia Central contractor Claiborne Mason to finish the Covington extension. This meant laying tracks on the ten-mile stretch that Irish laborers had graded east of the town before the Civil War began. When the Covington extension opened, more than six hundred people greeted the first train from Richmond with "smiles of joy," according to the *Richmond Whig*. The crowd celebrated with a feast on the Alleghany courthouse grounds.[246]

Next, work resumed on the eight tunnels and linking tracks between Covington and White Sulphur Springs in Greenbrier County, West Virginia. Claiborne Mason took over at Lewis Tunnel, where laborers bored away "night and day, Sunday and week day," the *Richmond Whig* reported. Eventually, 150 of those men would be convicts from the state penitentiary in Richmond; one of them was the legendary John Henry.[247]

Denis Shanahan was now a Confederate army veteran. He settled with his immediate and extended family in Covington and worked as an advisor on the Mud Tunnel. Kelly's Tunnel, almost complete before the war, required only tracks, leaving John Kelly free to sign on as a Mud Tunnel contractor. The bore was so difficult that a temporary track around it was necessary. When the men finally holed through, passengers headed east on

A rare image of Virginia Central Railroad locomotive 33 at Jackson's River Station in Alleghany County, circa 1870. A little Irish boy stands on top. *Photograph from* Chessie's Road *by Charles W. Turner.*

the temporary rails could see the incomplete passage "brilliantly illuminated with scores of fantastic lanterns," as the *Richmond Whig* described the scene, "gotten up by Colonel John Kelly, one of the contractors, in honor of the fact that there was daylight through the tunnel."[248]

Last, after one year of discussion, the State of Virginia merged the Virginia Central with the Covington and Ohio Railroad in 1868. The result was the Chesapeake and Ohio Railway. Still deeply in debt, the state sold the new railroad to financier Collis P. Huntington. As part of the deal, Virginia conveyed its title for the Blue Ridge Tunnel to the Chesapeake and Ohio in 1870. In exchange, the Chesapeake and Ohio assumed more than $600,000 in bond debt from the state.[249]

Backed by Huntington's cash infusion, the newly merged railroad finished the four tunnels begun between Millboro and Covington before the Civil War. All other work was complete by January 22, 1873, when Claiborne Mason drove the final spike in Chesapeake and Ohio tracks near Huntington, West Virginia. Richmond was connected with the Ohio River by rail at last. The final cost was $1.6 million for the Blue Ridge Railroad, $2.6 million for the Covington and Ohio and $2.2 million for the Virginia Central.[250]

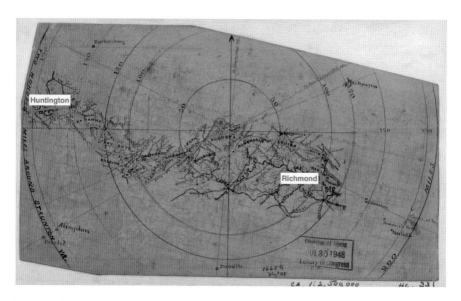

Richmond to Huntington map. The completed Virginia Central Railroad route to the Ohio River. *Courtesy of the Library of Congress.*

The first train on the finished line left Richmond for Huntington on the evening of January 23. It covered 423 miles and arrived to a one-hundred-gun salute. "The headlights of the engine appeared around the bend," the *Richmond Whig* reported, "and she rushed screaming into the town. The first train from Richmond to Huntington! To say that the occupants of that train were welcomed would be a feeble way of expressing the enthusiastic display. A yell burst forth as they came up to the platform and the passengers were almost dragged out by eager hands."[251]

The finished tracks made the Great Springs region of Virginia and West Virginia more accessible from all directions; passenger traffic on the Chesapeake and Ohio increased by 8 percent between 1872 and 1873. By this time, Virginia had returned some, though not all, of the money that it owed Kelly and Company for expenditures on the Brooksville and Blue Ridge Tunnels from March 1855 through February 1856. But for money the company spent from then until the Blue Ridge Tunnel opened in 1858, the state repaid with bonds still below stated value. In 1873, the state made a second refund of $10,491.97, including interest, to John Larguey's estate (he died in 1858) and to John Kelly. The partial refund may have given Kelly the impetus for still more railroad work. He returned to his former milieu in 1873 and began work on six sections of the Valley Railroad north of Staunton.[252]

Meanwhile, Kelly also focused on Sweet Chalybeate Springs. He opened the summer 1873 season with an advertisement that proclaimed, "Valuable as these waters are admitted to be when used as a beverage, the great charm of the place, pleasurably, hygienically, and medicinally, is found in the large enclosed pools for plunge bathing." Visitors to the Great Springs region were of no small importance to the financial health of struggling mountain communities in those postwar times. The railroad's broken bridges and twisted tracks were once visible proof of a divided nation. Now the railroad bolstered the economy as middle- and upper-class northerners flocked to the springs for escape from their industrial environs.[253] John Moorman, a travel writer, offered an itinerary:

> Travelers from the North or East to any of the principal Springs in the mountains of Virginia or West Virginia, to avail themselves most largely of railroad facilities, must necessarily make STAUNTON a point in their journey. From Staunton, the Rockbridge and Bath Alum, the Warm, Hot, Healing, White Sulphur, Salt, and Red Sulphur Springs, are conveniently reached by railroad with small amount of staging, and in the order here in which they are set down. The Sweet and Red Sweet are on the same general route, and are reached by a detour of seventeen miles from the White Sulphur.[254]

Travel through the Blue Ridge Tunnel was surprisingly safe, considering the narrow radius of the exit curve at the east portal. No one ever died from a train mishap, but the dark mountain vault seemed to invite desperate behavior through the decades. Local lore maintains that someone threw a baby out of a window while the train was in the passage and that the child is buried on the north side of the old track bed. In 1880, an escaped prisoner leapt from a freight car inside the tunnel. He lost a leg in the process. In 1910, an eighteen-year-old Italian immigrant was riding in a car with her family and other immigrants as the westbound train entered the Blue Ridge Tunnel. When engine smoke poured through the open windows, the half-asleep passengers panicked. As they stampeded toward the rear exit door, the young woman jumped off the train or was pushed. The car wheels cut her body in half.[255]

Earth slides, curse of the Blue Ridge Railroad construction in the 1850s, remained a threat over the years. In 1870, a heavy downpour destroyed the South River Bridge at Waynesboro shortly after a westbound train passed over. The same storm prevented an eastbound train from leaving the Blue Ridge Tunnel. Passengers were stranded overnight. The stretch between

Afton Depot and the tunnel's east portal was a persistent problem. A flood that damaged roads and canals throughout the state caused a heavy slide at the depot in 1877. As late as 1942, service was halted for two days when tons of earth and rocks rolled down the mountainside at the east portal.[256]

Despite landslides, the Blue Ridge Tunnel served well as a gateway to the Ohio River until World War II. Three factors led to the closing: increased traffic, a need for bigger locomotives should the government want to move troops and substantial deterioration of bricks on the west side. The Chesapeake and Ohio Railroad began grading for a replacement tunnel somewhat parallel to the old one in November 1941. Blue Ridge Railroad 1850s crews would have recognized construction methods at the new tunnel. They would have marveled, though, at the materials, equipment and speed of progress. The 1940s men worked in alternating ten-hour shifts, piercing the bore with dynamite. Each blasting operation consisted of a series of explosions that required seven hundred to nine hundred pounds of dynamite and removed ten feet of rock. Excavations at the west end were hauled in dump cars through the old tunnel to create an embankment on the east side.[257]

Just as in the 1850s, greenstone at the east portal of the new tunnel was stable. But supporting timber was needed for shoring up the west end while

Left: A muck car leaving the east portal during construction of the new Blue Ridge Tunnel, circa 1943. *Right*: The old Blue Ridge Tunnel. *From* Railway Age, *January 8, 1944.*

Right: During construction of the new Blue Ridge Tunnel, a cherry-picker device on the drill carriage raised empty muck cars up and out of the way. *From* Railway Age, *January 8, 1944.*

Below: Movable concrete form used to line the new Blue Ridge Tunnel. *From* Railway Age, *January 8, 1944.*

Opening day of the new Blue Ridge Tunnel, 1944. *Courtesy of Dale Brumfield.*

the men applied concrete twelve inches thick to the walls. Dynamite, air compressors for drilling, a large blower fan for ventilation and a generator to power the dump cars made construction supremely easier in the 1940s. Still, two workmen died, and a labor shortage caused by the war pushed the opening date forward by three months. The new Blue Ridge Tunnel is 4,230 feet long. It first received traffic on March 30, 1944, but the old tunnel was not forgotten. A year later, the *Richmond Times Dispatch* called it one of the seven wonders of Virginia.[258]

The Blue Ridge Railroad, especially the original Blue Ridge Tunnel, has had remarkable longevity in the public memory. More than three decades after its completion, Virginians were still in awe of the prosperity and ease of travel that trains had brought them. In a single issue in 1891, the *Times Dispatch* printed a twenty-article history of the project. "The Chesapeake and Ohio Railway is a monument to perseverance in the face of stupendous difficulties," the paper stated, recalling that "'Westward Ho!'" was the motto and the Ohio River was the goal of the road from the beginning."[259]

Hundreds of newspaper and periodical articles have been written about the Blue Ridge Railroad since 1849. Yet during these years, they have ignored, for the most part, the men who built it and Claudius Crozet's fitful relationship with them. Fortunately, a few of the laborers have lived on in family stories. For instance, a direct descendant of Remus Brackett always knew that he had a twin brother, Romulus. Research then revealed that Claudius Crozet's manager, William Sclater, leased the labor of both brothers to repair and finalize Blue Ridge Railroad tracks in 1854. The Brackett men were working for the railroad by the 1880s—one as a "hand" and the other as an "engineer," according to the census. It was gratifying to learn that they received wages for work they had done previously as forced-labor slaves.[260]

From oral family history repeated since the 1850s, one Irish American was aware that his great-great-grandfather, Patrick Hanley, was born on the Berehaven Peninsula in County Cork—home to at least five men working on the Blue Ridge Railroad. Like them, Patrick was likely employed in Berehaven copper mines when the Great Hunger began. After immigrating, he worked as a blaster at the Blue Ridge Tunnel. He moved with his family to a copper mine district in Michigan around 1856 and died later in a mining accident. It was likely a cave-in similar to ones at the Blue Ridge Railroad tunnels.[261]

An enduring memory of the Blue Ridge Railroad workers can be found in a folksong collected by Maud Karpeles, assistant for British and southern Appalachian folksong collector Cecil Sharp. In 1918, the pair

Construction of the rail-to-trail project leading to the Blue Ridge Tunnel east portal in Nelson County, Virginia, 2015. *Author's collection.*

Left: Replacement Blue Ridge Tunnel. *Right*: The rail-to-trail path to the old tunnel. *Author's collection.*

The rail-to-trail path at the entrance of the Blue Ridge Tunnel east portal in Nelson County, Virginia. *Author's collection.*

The rail-to-trail path inside the Blue Ridge Tunnel east portal in Nelson County, Virginia. *Author's collection.*

visited Rockfish Gap. They asked local people to sing eighteenth-century British ballads learned orally from parents or grandparents. The songsters, all members of the Fitzgerald family, included Clinton Fitzgerald and his wife, Florence.[262] Maud Karpeles returned to Rockfish Gap in September 1950. She was curious to know if any of the 1918 singers or their songs had survived. Florence Fitzgerald was widowed and remarried by this time. Karpeles wrote in her diary that she "spent a delightful afternoon with Mrs. Puckett (Florence Fitzgerald) & got 5 songs from her."[263]

One of the songs that Mrs. Puckett sang that afternoon was "Pat Do This, Pat Do That," a traditional Irish railroad workers' tune. The singer may have learned it from her mother, whose Ireland-born grandfather worked for the railroad in western Albemarle County in 1852. The lyrics provide a musical glimpse of life for Irish men laboring along countless tracks in America—in this case, the memorable Blue Ridge Railroad:[264]

> *Pat do this, and Pat do that*
> *Without our coats, without our hats*
> *Nothing in the world but an old straw hat to work out on the railroad*
> *Ruby shoogaroo, shooga rooga roo*

The Virginia Blue Ridge Railroad

Sugar in the cream pot, how do you do?
I'm just on the railroad fada fada ray
Johnny comes picking on the banjo
Railroad's done, we'll take a ride
Here we go, side by side
Here we go, side by side
Johnny comes picking on the banjo[265]

Watchman at the Blue Ridge Tunnel

*History of the Sheeler Family
by Gladys Wiltshire Burd*

David L. Sheeler and Susan G. Sheeler moved to the Blue Ridge Tunnel when Bettie the oldest child was just a baby, twelve more children were born there.

They lived in a four-room house, at the mouth of the tunnel, cooked on an open fire. They later built two more rooms, a kitchen and dining room, then they bought a cook stove.

Four Sheeler boys worked on the C&O Railroad at one time. Joe, John, and Doonce were brakemen at first, and later were conductors. Ashley was a fireman, he was called out one night and a fire around one of the wheels of the engine, he got down on the stops of the engine with a valve to put out the fire, and a breast bridge struck him in his chest and killed him.

Mr. Sheeler was the tunnel's watchman. He had to go through the tunnel from the West side, then from the East side to flag the trains. He did this for 22 years.

At times were four or five trains that had to be kept 10 minutes apart. His red light would stop one train until the tunnel was cleared.

One day a huge rock rolled down from the tunnel and on the tracks, a passenger train was due, no men were there at that time so Cassie Sheeler a daughter ran to Afton to get help. Mrs. Sheeler hurried up in the tunnel and laid torpedoes on the tracks to slow down the on coming

Left: North side of the watchman's house adjacent to tracks at the Blue Ridge Tunnel east portal, 1916. *Courtesy of the C&O Historical Society.*

train. Cassie found the section hands and they hurried back with her on a handcar, they relieved Mrs. Sheeler and they laid torpedoes all the way through the tunnel.

The section hands stopped the train just in time. They uncoupled the cars and left them on the other side of the tunnel. The engine slowly went through the tunnel and pushed the huge rock off on the side. The engine went back and brought the cars through.

The train master was on the train, the train never stopped at the house, but this time they did. The train master and others got off and thanked them for saving their lives.

Annie Sheeler only four years old was killed playing near the tunnel when a large rock rolled down and struck her. She only lived 20 minutes.

Mr. Sheeler slept in his clothes on a cot, kept his white and red lamps burning all night as he had to go out all hours to flag the trains. He did this for 22 years...Cassie Sheeler was my mother.[266]

"Births of Negroes"

After slave agent William U. Barton died, his account book was left at Brooksville, the home of his relative by marriage, George Farrow. Four pages in the book list the names and ages or birth dates of Brooksville slaves. Following is an exact transcription of the four pages.

Strother was born May 24 1809
Silas was born August 21 1809
Reuben was born 1809
Alfred was born 1803
Charles was born Sept 1828
Sam was born October 1828
Big Charles was born Mch 29 1817
Addison was born June 12 1833
Henry was born Oct 21 1818
Priscilla was born 1797
Amanda was born June 1 1840
Matilda was born 1812
Ned was born 1838
Davy was born 1845
Jesse was born Sept 1849
Sarah was born Aug 21 1818
Robert was born Nov 25 1841
Immanuel was born 1847

Ground radar has shown that a "street," possibly lined with slave quarters, was located half a mile north of Brooksville on George Farrow's property. *Author's collection.*

Susan was born Aug 1849
Benjamin was born June 1 1843
Mahala was born Sept 1833
Selena was born Mch 24 1824
Wallace was born May 4 1839
James was born Feby 1845
Stark was born July 1843
Cary was born Nov. 4 1834
Mary was born March 9, 1859
Matthias was born Jan 1859
Lucy was born Jan 17 1860
Nancy was born March 9. 1860
Lizzie Born aug 6. 1860
Fannie Born Sept 7. 1860
Henrietta Born oct 27. 1860
Tom Born Nov. 18. 1860

Bought Marshal & Family
Oct 2. 1860
—Marshal age—age 37 years
—Hardenia 34 "
—Maletus born 1856
—Bettie 1858.
—Mariah born 1859
Bertrand age 25 years cooper & blacksmith
Sam 24
Sally age 26
Liza age 24 bought in 1860
Moses 12 old
Bill 10 old
Susan 12 old
Matilda 14 old
Reuben 12 old
Lewis 8 years old
Jim 6 years old
Charles 8
Peter 22 years old
Ella age 4 years
Laura 6 years
Names of negroes belonging to George A. Farrow at the surrender of Gen Lee

Tables

Blue Ridge Railroad Pay Rates

Longevity may account for varying rates within a job category. Pay is per day unless otherwise noted.

	Before and after 1850 walkout	Early 1851	March 1851	Before April 1853 strike	After April 1853 strike	After summer 1853 demand	January 1854	December 1854	After March 1855 strike	After 1856 strike	1857
Boy	$0.75	$0.87½		$14/month or $0.54/day	$0.62	$0.75	$0.75	$0.75–$0.87½	$0.75–$1.00	$0.75–$0.87½–$1.00	$0.87½–$1.00
Floorer			$1.00	$1.00	$1.12½	$1.25	$1.25	$1.00	$1.00–$1.12½–$1.25	$1.00–$1.12½	$1.12½–$1.87½
Header				$1.16⅔–$1.25	$1.25	$1.37½ or $1.50 in tunnel center	$1.37½–$1.44	$1.25	$1.25	$1.25–$1.37½	$1.12½–$1.37½
Blaster				$1.25			$1.50	$1.25	$1.25	$1.25–$1.37½	$1.37½
Teamster				$1.00				$1.25	$0.87½–$1.00	$1.00	
Ostler								$1.12½			$1.12½
Waterman							$1.25	$1.00		$1.25	

	Before and after 1850 walkout	Early 1851	March 1851	Before April 1853 strike	After April 1853 strike	After summer 1853 demand	January 1854	December 1854	After March 1855 strike	After 1856 strike	1857
Dumper											$1.12½
Crew boss				$1.45½			$1.50–$1.58–$1.62½–$1.66	$1.50–$1.54		$1.50–$1.62½	$1.62½ $1.75
Blacksmith				$1.30			$1.42½–$1.47½	$1.30	$1.50		$1.42½ $1.50
Carpenter				$1.25			$1.25	$1.00–$1.25–$1.37½	$1.25–$1.75	$1.87½	$1.37½
Stone mason				$2.00				$2.00			$2.25
Overseer								$35/month			
Enslaved laborer	$125/year	$130/year					$1.12½	$1.12½			
Enslaved blacksmith							$1.12½	$1.40	$1.30	$1.42½	

Laborers Who Bored through the Blue Ridge Tunnel

Workers on both sides of the Blue Ridge Tunnel bored through the mountain on Monday, December 29, 1856. Following are the names of the men and boys who contributed to this momentous event, their jobs and the daily pay rate. Many of them, including one boy, worked two shifts, or sixteen hours straight. Three floorers worked three shifts in a row. Men whose job was listed as "water" manned water pumps.

Name	Job	Pay rate	Shifts	Side
John Fitzpatrick	boss	$1.62½	¼	east
Peter Sullivan	header	$1.37½	2	east
Edward Glavin	blaster	$1.37½	2	east
Richard Fitzgerald	header	$1.37½	2	east
Stephen Brien	floorer	$1.12½	2	east
Michael Collins	boy	$1.00	2	east
Michael Mahoney	boss	$1.75	1	east
John Savage	smith	$1.42½	1	east
John Savage	smith helper	$1.27½	1¾	east
John Bowen	carpenter	$1.27½	2	east
John Mullins	smith helper	$1.12½	1	east
William Kidney	ostler	$1.12½	1	east
Patrick Crowley	boss	$1.75	2	west
John Callanan	water	$1.12½	1½	west
Tim Donovan	water	$1.12½	2	west
Jeremiah Hanan	water	$1.12½	1½	west
Tim Leary 1st	water	$1.12½	2	west
Tim Leary 2nd	water	$1.12½	2	west
David Nelligan	smith	$1.42½	1	west
Murty Driscoll	smith	$1.42½	1	west
John Driscoll 1st	smith helper	$1.12½	¼	west
George Summers	carpenter	$1.87½	1	west
John Aherne	ostler	$1.12½	1	west
John Cronin	header	$1.37½	1	west
Tim Bouhane	floorer	$1.12½	2	west

Name	Job	Pay rate	Shifts	Side
Tom Coughlan	floorer	$1.12½	¼	west
John Sullivan	floorer	$1.12½	1	west
Pat Connell	boss	$1.62½	1	west
John O'Brien 3rd	header	$1.37½	1	west
Charles Duggan	floorer	$1.12½	1	west
Tim Bouhane	floorer	$1.12½	2	west
Pat Connnell	boss	$1.62½	1	west
Jeremiah Pharasy	header	$1.37½	1	west
John O'Brien 3rd	header	$1.37½	1	west
John Halleran	header	$1.37½	1	west
Pat Sullivan	header	$1.37½	1	west
Dennis O'Brien	header	$1.37½	1	west
Bat [Bartholomew] Downey	boy	$0.87½	1	west
Bat Donovan	floorer	$1.12½	1	west
Dennis Mehegan	floorer	$1.12½	1	west
Michael Downey	floorer	$1.12½	1	west
Jeremiah O'Brien 2nd	floorer	$1.12½	1	west
Dan Murphy	boy	$0.75	1	west
Tim Hegarty	floorer	$1.12½	1	west
Owen Sullivan	boy	$0.87½	1	west
John Murphy 2nd	floorer	$1.12½	1	west
John Murray	header	$1.37½	1	west
John Pine	floorer	$1.12½	1	west
Pat Shea	boy	$0.75	1	west
Michael Hurly	header	$1.37½	1	west
Michael Connors	header	$1.37½	1	west
Jeremiah Sullivan	blaster	$1.37½	¼	west
Pat Sullivan 2nd	floorer	$1.12½	¼	west
Tim Duggan	floorer	$1.12½	¼	west
Con Downey	floorer	$1.12½	¼	west
Tom Hayes	floorer	$1.12½	¼	west
Jeremiah Delay	floorer	$1.12½	¼	west
John Driscoll	boy	$1.00	1¼	west
Jerry Kelly	boy	$1.00	¼	west
Dan Sullivan	boy	$0.75	¼	west

Name	Job	Pay rate	Shifts	Side
Tom Hennessey	floorer	$1.12½	¼	west
James Goolding	floorer	$1.12½	3	west
John Barrett	floorer	$1.12½	3	west
John Lehane	floorer	$1.12½	¼	west
John Hurley	floorer	$1.12½	3	west
James Murphy 2nd	floorer	$1.12½	¼	west
Pat Swinay [Sweeny]	floorer	$1.12½	¼	west
John Connors	floorer	$1.12½	¼	west
Pat Burke	floorer	$1.12½	¼	west
James Donovan	floorer	$1.12½	¼	west
Jeremiah Larguey	clerk	$1.37½	1	west
Pat Connors	floorer	$1.12½	1	west

Slave Labor on the Railroad, 1850—1861

BRR: Blue Ridge Railroad
VCR: Virginia Central Railroad

Year	Estimated number of men	Slaveholder, slave agent or supervisor	Railroad	Nature of the work	Location	County
1850–52	42–72	Mordecai Sizer	BRR	Cleared and grubbed land. Excavated stony ground, slate and solid rock. Made embankments. Built dry walls. Filled ravine with loose rock. Built culverts.	Sections 2, 3, 4 east of approach to the Blue Ridge Tunnel	Albemarle
1850–52	35+	T.J. Randolph	BRR	Cleared and grubbed land. Hauled rock. Built fifteen culverts.	Sections 7, 8 between Greenwood Tunnel and Blair Park	Albemarle
1851	2	William Withrow, Jr.	BRR	Delivered nails and cement.	Blue Ridge Tunnel	Augusta
1852	9	Robert F. Harris, brick maker	BRR	Cut 230 cords of wood. Loaded and hauled wood in wagons. Fired bricks in kiln.	Waynesboro	Augusta
1852	8	Stationmaster	VCR	Firemen and train hands at depot.	Woodville (now Ivy)	Albemarle
1852	1	William Ramsay	BRR	Delivered oil.	Blue Ridge Tunnel	Nelson
1853	Unknown	Unknown	BRR	Trimmed and ballasted tracks.	Road west to Greenwood Tunnel	Albemarle
1853	Unknown	Unknown	BRR	Cleared ditches. Additional ballasting.	Between Blair Park and Mechum's River depot	Albemarle
1853	1	William Withrow Jr.	BRR	Delivered and sold 4½ gallons tar.	Blue Ridge Tunnel	Augusta
1854	1	Unknown	BRR	Delivered shingles.	Blue Ridge Tunnel	Nelson

Year	Estimated number of men	Slaveholder, slave agent or supervisor	Railroad	Nature of the work	Location	County
1854	31	George Farrow, David Hansborough, William Ramsay	BRR	Blacksmithing. Cleared debris from tunnel floor. May have manned water pumps.	Blue Ridge Tunnel	Nelson
1854	37	William M. Sclater, slave scout and superintendent	BRR	Laid and ballasted four sections of track.	Sections intervening between temporary track sections	Albemarle Nelson Augusta
1854	37	Sclater's crew	BRR	Prepared all parts [13 miles] of Blue Ridge Railroad used by Virginia Central Railroad. Trimmed and ballasted all unfinished sections awaiting opening of Blue Ridge Tunnel.	Tracks from Mechum's Depot to Blue Ridge Tunnel	Albemarle Nelson
Late 1854	37	Sclater's crew	BRR	Ballasted and improved unfinished sections of the Blue Ridge Railroad to prepare for tracks.	Unknown	Albemarle Nelson Augusta
1856	1	David Hansborough	BRR	Delivered shingles.	Blue Ridge Tunnel	Nelson
1856	12	Charles Ellet	VCR	Maintenance of the temporary track.	Unknown	Albemarle Nelson Augusta
1857	1	James Bowen	BRR	Delivered steel, wick and fuse.	Blue Ridge Tunnel	Nelson
1860	6	John S. Cocke	VCR	Unknown	Unknown	Unknown
1861	6	John S. Cocke	VCR	Unknown	Unknown	Unknown

$\mathcal{V}$iolent $\mathcal{D}$eaths at the $\mathcal{B}$lue $\mathcal{R}$idge $\mathcal{T}$unnel

Vandalism and deteriorating bricks at the old Blue Ridge Tunnel west portal, 2014. *Author's collection.*

Name	Birthplace	Birth date	Job	Date of death	Cause according to death records	Place of burial
Branaman, first name unknown	Ireland	Unknown	Unknown	June 8, 1859	"Irishman killed in tunnel"	Unknown
Calden, Don	Ireland	Unknown	Unknown	January 21, 1851	"blown up in large tunnel"	Unknown
Cashman, Lewis	County Cork, Ireland	Unknown	header	possibly March 1854	Unknown	leg buried at Thornrose Cemetery
Connel, Michael	Ireland	Unknown	Unknown	September 9, 1850	"killed in tunnel"	Unknown
Conovan (or Donovan), Dan	County Cork, Ireland	1803	Unknown	December 30, 1857	"accidental"	Thornrose Cemetery
Curren, Michael	Ireland	Unknown	header	possibly 1854	"wounded by a blast" "lost both hands in explosion"	Unknown
Dacy (or Deasy), Dennis	County Cork, Ireland	1824	floorer	April 24, 1854	"by a fall"	Thornrose Cemetery
Devine, Thomas	Ireland	Unknown	Unknown	June 27, 1850	"blown up"	Unknown
Griffin, Morris	Ireland	1827	Unknown	January 21, 1851	"Irish blown up in large tunnel"	Unknown
Hurly, Mick	County Cork, Ireland	1827	header	June 8, 1859	"accidental blast of rock" "blowing rock" at the "Rockfish Tunnel"	Thornrose Cemetery
Mahaney (or Mahoney), Thomas	Ballymartle, County Cork, Ireland	1824	header	August 3, 1854	possibly murdered	Thornrose Cemetery
Malone, James	Ireland	Unknown	Unknown	September 3, 1850	"killed in tunnel"	Unknown
Sullivan, Dan	Ireland	Unknown	Unknown	March 5, 1856	"blasting rock"	Thornrose Cemetery
Sullivan, Dan	County Cork, Ireland	1829	floorer or header	April 19, 1853	"accidental sliding of earth"	Thornrose Cemetery

Notes

A Note on Sources

1. "Collections A to Z," http://www.virginiamemory.com/collections/ collections_a_to_z; Herrin, *America Transformed*, 150; Middleton, *Landmarks on the Iron Road*, 111; Garvey Winegar, "Crozet Tunnel Visited to Select Plaque Site," *Charlottesville Daily Progress*, July 28, 1976, B-1.

Preface

2. Dilts, *Great Road*, 133, 138.
3. Gleeson, *Irish in the South*, 2–3.
4. Ibid., 127.
5. Albemarle County court records and records kept by western Albemarle attorney John B. Spiece show only two court cases involving Irish and slaves during the construction decade. Neither slave is documented as a railroad laborer. In 1855, Fayette, a slave, was charged with attempting rape on Catherine Devine, an "Irish girl." He was tried and transported in 1856. In 1856, a slave named Harrison who lived on a plantation near the Greenwood Tunnel was charged with robbing an Irishman "on the highway." Court records indicate that the Irishman was Bartholomew O'Sullivan and that Harrison attacked him with a knife. When O'Sullivan failed to show up as a witness, the court

discharged Harrison. See *Guide to the Business Records of Firms Located in Albemarle County, VA, 1819–1902, 1848–1879*, Mss 38, Albert and Shirley Small Special Collections, University of Virginia; Towler, *Court Doth Order*, 168.

6. Ely, *Israel on the Appomattox*, 368–69; Gleeson, *Irish in the South*, 128. Bryan Giemza notes in "Turned Inside Out" that evidence of southern Irish and black alliances is "consistently inconsistent." The same may hold true for southern Irish and black labor conflict.

Chapter 1

7. James Poyntz Nelson, "Virginia Blue Ridge Railroad," n.d., C&O Predecessors Box III, Chesapeake and Ohio Railway Historical Society, Clifton Forge, VA.

8. Couper, *Southern Sketches*, 6–8, 9, 12, 19.

9. Ibid., 18, 20, 22.

10. Hunter and Dooley, *Claudius Crozet*, 14; Adams, *Dictionary of Virginia Biography*, 580–82; Claudius Crozet to Board of Public Works (hereafter BPW), April 1, 1850, Blue Ridge Railroad Papers, Library of Virginia (hereafter BRR). In 1850, Crozet's assistants carried their heavy surveying equipment until he hired slaves by the month to haul the instruments. He likely made the same arrangement for his own surveying trips.

11. Couper, *Southern Sketches*, 58.

12. Ibid., 56–57, 61, 71–72.

13. Ibid., 78; Coleman, "Virginia Central Railroad," 57.

14. Couper, *Southern Sketches*, 91–92.

15. Peyton, *History of Augusta County*, 221.

16. Ibid.

17. Claudius Crozet to BPW, November 30, 1849, BRR. New York, Pennsylvania, Maryland, Virginia, South Carolina and Georgia built rails and tunnels through the Appalachian Mountain chain in the 1840s and 1850s.

18. Hunter and Dooley, *Claudius Crozet*, 140–41.

19. *Richmond Daily Dispatch*, "Virginia Blue Ridge Tunnels and Railroad," January 28, 1857.

Chapter 2

20. Federal Census, Fluvanna County, VA, 1850; Federal Census Slave Schedule, Fluvanna County, VA, 1850.

21. Familysearch.org, Ancestral File KCCT-9G, https://familysearch.org/pal:/MM9.2.1/MZ6R-Z6S; Ronald Ray Turner, Prince William County, VA, *Clerk's Loose Papers 4. Selected Transcripts 1811–1899 Miscellaneous Records* (Manassas, VA: R.R. Turner, 2004), 57, 71, http://www.pwcvabooks.com/pwcvabookspublishedworks.

22. Mark Auslander, "Enslaved Labor and Building the Smithsonian: Reading the Stones," *Southern Spaces*, December 12, 2012, http://www.southernspaces.org/2012/enslaved-labor-and-building-smithsonian-reading-stones; Francis X. Clines, "The Closing of a Circle," *New York Times*, January 10, 2009, A32, http://www.nytimes.com/2009/01/20/opinion/20tue4; Barton, Account Book; McInnis, *Slaves Waiting for Sale*, 99.

23. Mary E. Lyons, "Brooksville African American Community, 1850–1880," unpublished compilation, 2013; Central Virginia History Researchers, "African-American Families Database," http://www.centralvirginiahistory.org.

24. Federal Census Slave Schedule, Albemarle County, VA, 1850; Will Book 14: 430, Albemarle County, VA; Claudius Crozet to BPW, August 2, 1853, BRR.

25. Claudius Crozet to BPW, August 2, 1853, BRR; McInnis, *Slaves Waiting for Sale*, 75; E.C. Howard to Claudius Crozet, June 20, 1852, BRR.

26. Claudius Crozet to BPW, December 9, 1853, and January 4, 1854, BRR; contracts for slave labor, BRR; John Wood Jr. to the BPW, April 20, 1854, BRR; William Sclater affidavit for BPW, October 28, 1864, BRR; W.P. Bocark, "Opinion for the Board of Public Works," November 1, 1854, BRR; William Wallace store ledger, Greenwood, VA, January 1854, private collection.

27. Claudius Crozet to BPW, December 6, 1853, January 4, 1854, December 1, 1854, December 28, 1854, BRR.

28. Blue Ridge Tunnel payrolls, BRR; Bocark, "Opinion"; BPW, Journal L, July 4, 1853–June 7, 1855, Library of Virginia (hereafter LV).

29. Federal Census, Albemarle County, VA, 1850; contracts for slave labor, 1854–1855, BRR; Blue Ridge Tunnel payrolls, BRR; BPW, Journal L, July 4, 1853–June 7, 1855, LV.

30. Federal Census, Alleghany County, VA, 1860; *Annual Report of the President and Directors of the Virginia Central Railroad*, 1853–59.

31. Virginia Central Railroad Papers, Library of Virginia (hereafter VCR); *Civil Engineer and Architect's Journal* 20 (1857): 191; Albemarle County, VA Fiduciary Book 4, 382. Data extracted by Sam Towler.

32. VCR; descendant of Lewis Harvey to the author, October 17, 2013; Albemarle County Court Records Index—Civil War Era, Library of Virginia, 23, 110.

Chapter 3

33. O'Brien, "Factory, Church, and Community," 520, 526.
34. Laxton, *Famine Ships*, 50.
35. *New York Times*, "163 Years Later, a President Visits to Say Thank You," May 23, 2010, MB1; "Museum to Present Lecture on USS *Jamestown's* Voyage to Ireland April 3," https://www.quinnipiac.edu/news-and-events/museum-to-present-lecture-on-uss-jamestowns-voyage-to-ireland-april-3/; Laxton, *Famine Ships*, 51–52.
36. Laxton, *Famine Ships*, 51–52.
37. Scally, *End of Hidden Ireland*, 44–45.
38. Ibid., 167, 168; Dunn, *Ballykilcline Rising*, 27.
39. Duffy, *Killing of Major Denis Mahon*, 121.
40. Mary Lee Dunn, "Bishop's List," compilation of tenants evicted by Denis Mahon originally published in George Joseph Plunket Browne's letter to Earl of Shrewsbury, *Freemans Journal* (Dublin, Ireland), April 28, 1848; Saint Francis of Assisi Church records, *Valley of the Shadow: Two Communities in the Civil War*, Virginia Center for Digital History, University of Virginia (hereafter VS), http://valley.lib.virginia.edu; Doyle, "Remaking of Irish America," 213.

Chapter 4

41. Couper, *Southern Sketches*, 128; Coleman, "Virginia Central Railroad," 59.
42. Familysearch.org, Ancestral File Number KCCT-9G, https://familysearch.org/pal:/MM9.2.1/MZ6R-Z6S.
43. Coleman, "Virginia Central Railroad," 61; *Irish American Weekly*, "Great Tunnel," September 21, 1849, 4.
44. *Baltimore Sun*, September 29, 1849.
45. *Frank Leslie's Chimney Corner*, "Self-made Man of Our Times, John Kelly" 17 (1873): 231; Kelly's 1850 letter to the governor of Virginia was articulate and written in a fine hand, showing that his education went beyond the basic level implied in the biography; Tithe Applotment Books

1823–1837 for Rathcooney, County Cork, National Archives, Dublin, Ireland; Lewis, *Topographical Dictionary of Ireland*.

46. *Frank Leslie's Chimney Corner*, "Self-made Man," 214; *Baltimore Sun*, "Mortuary Notice," July 9, 1887.

47. James Sykes recommendation letter, October 4, 1849, BRR; Cornelius Kelly to Claudius Crozet, October 11, 1849, BRR.

48. Christopher Valentine to Thomas Jefferson Randolph, December 20, 1849, Albert and Shirley Small Special Collections, Library of Virginia, accession number 8937-b; Hunter and Dooley, *Claudius Crozet*, 144. The authors incorrectly state that Thomas Jefferson Randolph's sections seven and eight extended to Mechum's River.

49. Claudius Crozet to BPW, October 5, 1850, BRR; "Thomas Jefferson Randolph," http://www.monticello.org/site/jefferson/thomas-jefferson-randolph; Federal Census Slave Schedule, Albemarle County, VA, 1850, 1860; Thomas Jefferson Randolph, "To the Editors of the *Richmond Daily Times*," *Richmond Daily Times*, March 13, 1850; Valentine to Randolph, 1849.

50. Federal Census Slave Schedule, Albemarle County, VA, 1850; Thomas Jefferson Randolph to Claudius Crozet, October 15, 1849, BRR; Laura Armitage, "Miscellaneous Notes and Data," Blue Ridge Railroad–Blue Ridge Tunnel Box, Chesapeake and Ohio Historical Society, Clifton Forge, VA.

51. Federal Census Slave Schedule, Albemarle County, VA, 1850.

52. Coleman, "Virginia Central Railroad," 62, 70.

53. Valentine to Randolph, 1849; Brooksville Tunnel payrolls, BRR. According to Valentine and Randolph, they had an understanding with the Board of Public Works whereby the state would employ Randolph's slave crew elsewhere along the line should they finish sections seven and eight ahead of time. The partners claimed a loss of $1,000 income when the railroad failed to honor the agreement. The Board of Public Works declined to pay compensation. See BPW, Journal L, LV.

54. *Thirty-ninth Annual Report of the Board of Public Works to the General Assembly of Virginia with the Accompanying Documents*, Richmond, VA, 1855, 775.

55. *Baltimore Sun*, "Twenty Dollars Reward," September 19, 1848, 4; Claudius Crozet, Blue Ridge Tunnel comparative estimates, January 21, 1850, BRR.

56. Crozet, comparative estimates, BRR.

57. Claudius Crozet to BPW, January 1, 1858, cited in Couper, *Southern Sketches*, 167.

58. *Staunton Spectator*, "Contractors and Road Hands," February 6, 1850.

59. Ibid., "Fugitive Slaves," February 15, 1850.

60. Ibid.

Chapter 5

61. Ibid., "Railroad Hands," February 15, 1850.

62. *Staunton Vindicator*, "Irish Commotion," February 18, 1850.

63. Ibid.

64. Ibid.; *Staunton Vindicator*, "The Irish Trials," March 4, 1850.

65. *Staunton Spectator*, "The Rioters," March 27, 1850.

66. Megan Davis, "Tunnel Vision," *Charlottesville Daily Progress*, April 10, 2010, A1; Fogarty, *Commonwealth Catholicism*, 135; Couper, *Southern Sketches*, 132.

67. Way, *Common Labour*, 194; Donnelly, *Captain Rock*, 167; Perry, "Shillelaghs, Shovels, and Secrets," 55–56.

68. Claudius Crozet to BPW, October 5, 1850, BRR.

69. *Staunton Spectator*, "Blue Ridge Rail-road," March 27, 1850.

70. Ibid.

71. Ibid.; *Staunton Spectator*, March 23, 1850.

72. *Staunton Spectator*, "Irish Laborers," August 9, 1854; *Staunton Vindicator*, "Irish Liberality," August 28, 1854; Ron Michener, Department of Economics, University of Virginia, to the author, August 21, 2014.

73. Claudius Crozet to BPW, May 6, 1850, BRR. The pay rate of $0.75 a day is based on a reference in Crozet's letter to BPW, November 4, 1851.

74. Ibid.

75. Ibid.

76. Ibid.

77. Ibid.; Lyons, *Blue Ridge Tunnel*, 17.

Chapter 6

78. Claudius Crozet to BPW, November 15, 1850, BRR.

79. John Kelly to John B. Floyd, November 15, 1850, BRR.

80. Ronald Ray Turner, *Prince William County Clerks Loose Papers* 3 (1998), 44, 57, Prince William County, Virginia, http://www.pwcvabooks.com.

81. Claudius Crozet to James Brown Jr., June 18, 1850, BRR.

82. *Guide to the Business Records*, Mss 38; Federal Census, Augusta County, VA, 1850.
83. Claudius Crozet to James Brown Jr., June 18, 1850, BRR; *Daily (Montgomery) Alabama Journal*, May 22, 1850; *Daily National Intelligencer* (Washington, D.C.), May 13, 1850; *Daily (St. Louis) Missouri Republican*, May 26, 1850.
84. *Staunton Spectator*, June 18, 1850; Way, *Common Labour*, 216.
85. Transcription of W.B. Alexander coffin record book, circa 1995, Public Library, Waynesboro, VA; Federal Census, Augusta County, VA, 1850.
86. Claudius Crozet to BPW, October 5, 1850, BRR.
87. Ibid.
88. Brooksville Tunnel payrolls, BRR; Wooley and Ratz, *Rock Fences of the Bluegrass*, 93–94. Masons at Brooksville Tunnel included Irishman John Quinn, the highest-paid laborer on the Blue Ridge Railroad, and local men George and Jake Hippert.
89. Blue Ridge Tunnel payrolls, BRR; Lyons, *Blue Ridge Tunnel*, 41; Way, *Common Labour*, 141; Claudius Crozet to BPW, October 5, 1850, BRR; BPW, Journal L, LV.

Chapter 7

90. Claudius Crozet to BPW, January 15, 1851; Valentine to Randolph, 1849.
91. Claudius Crozet to BPW, January 15, 1851.
92. Ibid.
93. Claudius Crozet to BPW, August 2, 1853, BRR; Lyons, "Blue Ridge Railroad Community," unpublished compilation; Lyons, "Blue Ridge Tunnel Payrolls," unpublished compilation; Way, *Common Labour*, 134.
94. Crozet to BPW, January 15, 1851, BRR.
95. Ibid.; Ellet, *Mountain Top Track*, 8.
96. Coleman, "Virginia Central Railroad," 64; Virginia Military Institute Archives, http://www.vmi.edu/archives; D. Walton, J.R.K. Co. recommendation letter, October 26, 1849, BRR; Federal Census, Nelson County, VA, 1850; Federal Census, Rockbridge County, VA, 1870. Timothy Ives and Co. soon assumed section eleven while contractors Collins and Baskins, followed by Jonathan Browning, took over section twelve. Meantime, the Blue Ridge Railroad paid for work, including culverts, on sections thirteen through sixteen. Presumably, these proceeded

west after the South River Bridge; the Virginia Central Railroad later reimbursed the state for the expense. See BPW, Journal L, LV.

97. Transcription of W.B. Alexander coffin record book, circa 1995, Public Library, Waynesboro, VA; Lyons, "Blue Ridge Tunnel Payrolls," unpublished compilation.

98. Couper, *Southern Sketches*, 133.

99. Blue Ridge Railroad account book, BRR; Department of the Army, *Technical Manual Military Explosives*, 1984, revised 1987, 2–5.

100. Holladay, "Diary," 17–18.

101. William U. Barton, Account Book, "Births of Negroes"; Lyons, "Brooksville African-American Community, 1850–1880"; Federal Census Slave Schedule, Albemarle County, VA, 1860, "slave houses" column. Brooksville slave family group surnames were Ailstock, Cross, Rodes, Spears, Stewart and White.

102. Holladay, "Diary," 18, 20; Lyons, "Blue Ridge Railroad Vendors."

103. Towler, "New York, Albemarle and Surrounding Farms"; Federal Census, Albemarle County, VA, 1850; Towler, "New York," unpublished manuscript, [16]; Federal Census, Albemarle County, VA, 1860. Towler's research on Brooksville documents a boardinghouse that fronted the turnpike on George Farrow's property, and the 1850 census suggests that a dwelling with fifty-four Irish residents was in the immediate vicinity of the Brooksville house.

104. Majewski, *A House Dividing*, 67; Federal Census Agricultural Schedule, Albemarle County, VA, 1850, 1860; Lyons, "Blue Ridge Railroad Vendors"; Blue Ridge Railroad account book, BRR; Federal Census Slave Schedule, Albemarle County, VA, 1850, 1860; personal property tax records, Albemarle County, VA, 1865.

105. Holladay, "Diary," 22.

106. Ibid.

107. National Archives of Ireland, Census of Ireland, 1901, House and Building Return.

108. Holladay, "Diary," 22.

109. Coleman, "Virginia Central Railroad," 48. Farish may have been William P. Farish, an Albemarle County farmer. Wright may have been William Wright from Scottsville in Albemarle County. The black train hands were Dennis, Dick and Tilman. The firemen were Andrew, Curtis, David and Ellick.

110. Blue Ridge Tunnel Payrolls, BRR.

111. E.C. Howard to Crozet, June 30, 1852, BRR.

112. Way, *Common Labour*, 138; Mordecai Sizer invoice, May 1852, BRR; Crozet to BPW, November 4, 1851, BRR; "Virginia Marriages 1851–1929," Ancestry.com. George A. Farrow became contractor for Sizer's sections two and three. Robert P. Smith later assumed these same sections. See BPW, Journal L, LV.

113. Blue Ridge Tunnel payrolls, BRR.

114. Ellet, *Mountain Top Track*, 9; Coleman, "Virginia Central Railroad," 49.

Chapter 8

115. Hobbs, *Canal on the James*, 14, 23; Derby and White, *National Cyclopedia of American Biography*, 360.

116. Ellet, *Mountain Top Track*, 2.

117. Nelson, *Chesapeake and Ohio*, 142, 144; Claudius Crozet to BPW, January 1, 1858; Middleton, *Landmarks on the Iron Road*, 111; Ellet, *Mountain Top Track*, 11. Nelson's map of the temporary track omits the detour around Kelly's Cut.

118. Ellet, *Mountain Top Track*, 10; Claudius Crozet to BPW, November 30, 1849.

119. Hunter and Dooley, *Claudius Crozet*, 151; Claudius Crozet to BPW, December 6, 1853, BRR; Claudius Crozet to BPW, November 30, 1849; Ellet, *Mountain Top Track*, 11.

120. Ellet, *Mountain Top Track*, 10; Hunter and Dooley, *Claudius Crozet*, 147.

121. Augusta County Register of Deaths, 1853–96, microfilm roll 102, LV; Blue Ridge Tunnel payrolls, BRR; Thornrose Cemetery record book.

122. Claudius Crozet to BPW, April 19, 1853, BRR.

123. Ibid.

124. Ibid.

125. Ibid.

126. Nelson, *Chesapeake and Ohio*, 56–58; Charles Ellet, *Thirty-eighth Annual Report of the Board of Public Works to the General Assembly of Virginia with the Accompanying Documents 1853–1854*, 536; *Richmond Daily Dispatch*, "Railroad Hands Wanted," April 27, 1853.

127. "History of St. Francis of Assisi Parish Part 2: The Founding of St. Francis, 1845. Father Daniel Downey Gets a Parish Start," http://www.stfrancisparish.org/hist2; Blue Ridge Tunnel payrolls, BRR.

128. Claudius Crozet to BPW, August 2, 1853, BRR.

129. Coleman, "Virginia Central Railroad," 79.

130. *Richmond Daily Dispatch*, July 15, 1853.

131. Claudius Crozet to BPW, August 2, 1853, BRR.

132. Ibid.

133. Blue Ridge Tunnel payroll, east side, July 1853, BRR; Augusta County Register of Deaths, 1853–96.

134. Gary Rogers, diagram, "Tunnel Vision," *Roanoke Times*, March 13, 2005, 2; Claudius Crozet to BPW, August 2, 1853, BRR.

135. Ibid.

136. Claudius Crozet to BPW, November 1853, BRR.

137. Trautwine, *Civil Engineer's Pocket Book*, 521–22.

138. Ibid.

139. Claudius Crozet to BPW, August 2, 1853, BRR; Scott Reynolds Nelson describes Mason in *Steel Drivin' Man* as a "resourceful but hard hearted man." Following orders from Robert E. Lee, the contractor captured Confederate army deserters in western Albemarle County and hanged them.

140. Claudius Crozet to BPW, August 2, 1853, BRR.

141. Ibid.

142. Ibid., November 1853, BRR.

143. Ibid., August 2, 1853, BRR; Hunter and Dooley, *Claudius Crozet*, 201. The Greenwood Tunnel plaque is now displayed on the grounds of the Virginia Military Institute.

144. *Alexandria Gazette*, "Central Railroad," December 7, 1853; Claudius Crozet to BPW, November 1853, BRR.

145. Claudius Crozet to BPW, November 1853, BRR.

146. Ibid.

147. Ibid.; Claudius Crozet to BPW, January 4, 1854, BRR.

148. Claudius Crozet to BPW, August 2, 1853, BRR; Claudius Crozet to BPW, November 1853, BRR.

149. Claudius Crozet to BPW, December 6, 1853.

Chapter 9

150. Claudius Crozet to BPW, January 4, 1854, BRR.

151. Ibid.

152. Ibid.; *Richmond Daily Dispatch*, August 28, 1852; *Richmond Daily Dispatch*, January 12, 1859; http://www.racetimeplace.com/ugrr/stillnarrative. After Toler and Cook dissolved their partnership in December 1854, they established separate offices in the heart of Richmond's slave-trading

district and continued their lucrative hiring out of enslaved cooks, bakers, wet nurses, washerwomen, carpenters, ostlers and so forth. See *Richmond Daily Dispatch*, January 16, 1855, and May 1, 1856.

153. Contract for Negro Slaves, December 23, 1853, BRR.

154. Ibid.; Blue Ridge Tunnel payrolls, 1854, BRR; Claudius Crozet to BPW, January 4, 1854, BRR.

155. Blue Ridge Tunnel payrolls, BRR; Lyons, "Blue Ridge Railroad Community"; Claudius Crozet to BPW, January 4, 1854, BRR.

156. Crozet to BPW, December 9, 1855; Couper, *Southern Sketches*, 160; Crozet to BPW, January 4, 1854; contracts for slave labor, January 9, 1854, BRR.

157. Federal Census, Albemarle County, 1850; receipt for payment of Maria Evans's service as cook to William Sclater, witnessed and signed by William Graves, Graves Accounting Part 4, William Graves Papers, Wisconsin Historical Society, Madison, WI; Claudius Crozet to BPW, December 6, 1853, BRR.

158. Wallace store ledger, January 1854; Bocark, "Opinion"; Crozet to BPW, May 2, 1854, BRR.

159. Claudius Crozet to BPW, January 4, 1854, BRR.

160. Ibid.

161. Coleman, "Virginia Central Railroad," 102; Claudius Crozet to BPW, December 9, 1855; Ellet, *Mountain Top Track*, 13.

162. Coleman, "Virginia Central Railroad," 144.

163. Ellet, *Mountain Top Track*; Couper, *Southern Sketches*, 141.

164. James Alexander, *Charlottesville Jeffersonian Republican*, March 22, 1854; *Lexington Gazette*, March 30, 1854.

165. Bocark, "Opinion."

166. Ibid.; John Wood Jr. to Claudius Crozet, April 20, 1854, BRR.

167. Bocark, "Opinion." Witnesses included Mr. Murray, the engineman; William Sclater; Samuel White; Robert P. Smith; Thomas W. Woods, Andrew Woods's brother; and Claudius Crozet.

168. Bocark, "Opinion"; Couper, *Southern Sketches*, 142.

169. Thornrose Cemetery record book; Blue Ridge Tunnel payrolls, BRR; Nelson, *Chesapeake and Ohio*, 89–90; Augusta County Register of Deaths, 1853–96.

170. *Staunton Vindicator*, "Who Are the Victims of Cholera?" August 14, 1854.

171. *New York Times*, "Oyster—Guilty or Not Guilty of Poison?" October 30, 1854; *Staunton Vindicator*, "Cholera in Richmond," July 17, 1854; *Staunton Spectator*, "Cholera at Richmond," July 26, 1854.

172. *Staunton Spectator*, "Cholera at Scottsville," July 12, 1854; *Staunton Vindicator*, "Cholera at the Tunnel," August 7, 1854; Blue Ridge Railroad ledger, 1851–57, BRR.

173. Way, *Common Labour*, 157; Blue Ridge Tunnel payrolls, BRR; Augusta County Register of Deaths, 1853–96; Thornrose Cemetery record book.

174. Janet Monge, University of Pennsylvania Museum of Archaeology and Anthropology, http://www.penn.museum/research/physical-anthropology/813-dead-men-of-duffys-cut.html; Claudius Crozet to James Alexander, July 31, 1854. Reprinted in the *Staunton Vindicator*, August 7, 1854.

175. *Staunton Spectator*, "The Cholera at the Tunnel," August 9, 1854.

176. *Staunton Vindicator*, "Cholera at the Tunnel," August 7, 1854.

177. Augusta County Register of Deaths, 1853–96; Transcription of W. Alexander coffin record book, circa 1995, Public Library, Waynesboro, VA; Thornrose Cemetery record book.

178. Claudius Crozet to BPW, November 5, 1854, BRR.

179. Ibid.

180. William Sclater to BPW, November 1, 1854, BRR.

181. Claudius Crozet to BPW, November 5, 1854, BRR.

182. Blue Ridge Tunnel payrolls, 1854, BRR; Claudius Crozet to BPW, December 1, 1854, BRR.

183. Claudius Crozet to BPW, December 1, 1854, BRR.

184. Ibid.

185. Claudius Crozet to BPW, December 28, 1854, BRR.

186. Ibid.

Chapter 10

187. Claudius Crozet to BPW, December 9, 1855, BRR; Brooksville Tunnel payrolls, BRR. Extant Brooksville Tunnel payrolls show that about 235 individuals worked in the passage or on the adjacent embankment between March 1854 and November 1856.

188. *Richmond Daily Dispatch*, February 2, 1855.

189. *Thirty-ninth Annual Report of the Board of Public Works to the General Assembly of Virginia with the Accompanying Documents*, 1855, xx.

190. *Annual Reports of the Internal Improvement Companies of the State of Virginia to the Board of Public Works, for the Year 1873* (Richmond, 1874), 174–75.

191. Claudius Crozet to BPW, March 2, 1855, cited in Couper, *Southern Sketches*, 144.

192. Claudius Crozet to BPW, March 1855, cited in Hunter and Dooley, *Claudius Crozet*, 157; Blue Ridge Tunnel payrolls, BRR. The Brooksville blacksmiths were Abraham, Robert Mickums and Thomas Barns.

193. Claudius Crozet to BPW, December 9, 1855, BRR.

194. Eugene Quinn, headstone, Quinn Cemetery, Albemarle County, VA; BPW, Journal L, LV; Brooksville Tunnel payrolls, BRR; Blue Ridge Tunnel payrolls, BRR; *Charlottesville Advocate*, August 5, 1855, reprinted as "Cholera at the Tunnel," in *Alexandria Gazette*, August 6, 1855.

195. *Richmond Daily Dispatch*, "Cholera Report Contradicted," August 8, 1855.

196. Claudius Crozet to BPW, December 9, 1855, BRR.

197. *Eighteenth Annual Report of the President and Directors of the Virginia Central Railroad Company to the Stockholders, at Their Annual Meeting, on the 10th November 1853* (Richmond, VA: Colin and Nowlan, 1853), 10.

198. Blue Ridge Railroad ledger, BRR; Claudius Crozet to BPW, December 9, 1855, BRR.

199. Blue Ridge Railroad ledger, BRR; Hunter and Dooley, *Claudius Crozet*, 157 and 203 note 9, referring to Crozet to BPW, June 16, 1856, BRR; Thornrose Cemetery record book; Blue Ridge Tunnel payrolls, BRR.

200. Morton, *Annals of Bath County*, 182; *Seventeenth Annual Report of the President and Directors of the Virginia Central Railroad to the Stockholders at Their Annual Meeting* [1857].

201. *Richmond Daily Dispatch*, "Excursion to Millboro," July 31, 1856.

202. Ibid.

203. Brooksville Tunnel payrolls, BRR; Crozet to BPW, January 1, 1858, cited in Couper, *Southern Sketches*, 166.

204. *Annual Report of the President and Directors of the Virginia Central Railroad to the Stockholders at Their Annual Meeting*, October 15, 1856.

205. Ellet, *Mountain Top Track*, 5.

206. Couper, *Southern Sketches*, 160–61.

207. *Richmond Times Dispatch*, "Blue Ridge Tunnel," January 1, 1857.

Chapter 11

208. Waddell, *Annals of Augusta County*, 448–49.

209. *Richmond Daily Dispatch*, "The Virginia Blue Ridge Tunnels and Railroad," January 28, 1857.

210. Ibid. According to BPW, Journal L, Claudius Crozet ordered "two marble slabs with inscription for the portal of the tunnel" from John T.

Rogers of Richmond in November 1851. The plaque is now housed at the Virginia Military Institute in Lexington, VA.

211. *Staunton Spectator*, March 18, 1857; Thornrose Cemetery record book; *Lexington Gazette*, March 19, 1857, cited in Couper, *Southern Sketches*, 161.

212. Barton, Account Book, "Births of Negroes"; Couper, *Southern Sketches*, 172; *Staunton Spectator*, July 15, 1857. Denis Shanahan's wife, Anne Marie Lyons Larguey, was John Larguey's adopted daughter.

213. *Charlottesville Advocate* editorial reprinted in *Lexington Gazette*, July 30, 1857, cited in Couper, *Southern Sketches*, 162.

214. Reprinted in the *Lexington Gazette* from the *Richmond Times Dispatch*, August 6, 1857, cited in Couper, *Southern Sketches*, 163; Nelson, *Chesapeake and Ohio*, 150; Claudius Crozet to BPW, January 1, 1858, BRR, cited in Couper, *Southern Sketches*, 170; Blue Ridge Railroad Account Book, BRR.

215. Blue Ridge Tunnel Payrolls, BRR; H.D. Whitcomb to the president and directors of the Virginia Central Railroad, September 21, 1857, VCR.

216. H.D. Whitcomb to the president and directors of the Virginia Central Railroad, September 21, 1857, VCR.

217. Ibid.

218. *Lexington Gazette*, "Brilliant Achievement at the Tunnel," October 27, 1857.

219. *American Railroad Journal*, November 10, 1857.

220. Claudius Crozet to BPW, January 1, 1858, cited in Couper, *Southern Sketches*, 172.

221. Crozet to Thomas H. DeWitt, January 11, 1858, cited in Hunter and Dooley, *Claudius Crozet*, 164.

222. *New York Herald*, 1857, reprinted in *Richmond Semi-Weekly Examiner*, December 1, 1857, cited in Coleman, "Virginia Central Railroad," 152.

223. Couper, *Southern Sketches*, 172; Crozet to DeWitt, February 8, 1858, cited in Hunter and Dooley, *Claudius Crozet*, 163.

224. Hunter and Dooley, *Claudius Crozet*, 163–64.

225. Blue Ridge Railroad payrolls, BRR; Couper, *Southern Sketches*, 172; James Alexander, *Charlottesville Jeffersonian Republican*, April 1858, reprinted in *Staunton Spectator*, December 31, 1858.

226. Herrin, *America Transformed*, 150; Coleman, "Virginia Central Railroad," 74; PRIIA 305-003/Amtrak 964 Technical Specification Initial Release (Amtrak, 2011), 11.

227. Claudius Crozet to BPW, January 1, 1858, cited in Couper, *Southern Sketches*, 171; W.B. Alexander coffin record book; Thornrose Cemetery record book.

228. Aquila Johnson Peyton, "Diary of Aquila Johnson Peyton," 1859–1861, microfilm 646, Albert and Shirley Small Special Collections, University of Virginia.

229. Federal Census, Augusta County, VA, 1860; Tax Assessment List, Augusta County, VA, 1865.

230. Federal Census, Albemarle County and Augusta County, VA, 1860; *Staunton Vindicator*, August 10, 1860, 2, VS.

231. Annual Report of the Board of Public Works, November 1859, XLVII; Nelson, *Chesapeake and Ohio*, 149–50; Watson, *Chesapeake and Ohio Tunnels*, 27–45; Blue Ridge Tunnel payrolls, BRR; Federal Census, Alleghany County, VA, 1860. Chesapeake and Ohio Railway records misspelled John Kelly's tunnel as Kelley's Tunnel. I use the spelling by which John Kelly consistently signed his correspondence. The same spelling appears on the tunnel portals. Kelly's former Blue Ridge Railroad workers included Callaghan Gorman, Michael Gorman, Michael Quinlan, John Pine, James O'Brien and John Long.

232. Turner, *Chessie's Road*, 47; Federal Census, Alleghany County, VA, 1860; American Civil War Soldiers Database, Ancestry.com; Nelson, *Chesapeake and Ohio*, 9.

Chapter 12

233. Robertson, *Stonewall Jackson*, 217–18.

234. Ibid.

235. Ibid., 369.

236. Drinker, *Tunneling, Explosives, and Rock Drills*, 886–88.

237. Turner, *Chessie's Road*, 60.

238. Edmund Fontaine, "[T]o the Farmers Residing in the Vicinity of the Virginia Central Railroad," broadside, September 2, 1863, HathiTrust Digital Library, hathitrust.org.

239. Scheele, "'Oh Luce,'" 89–90. Commas have been inserted for clarity where needed. "Mr. Bowen" was James Bowen, owner of Mirador plantation. Mary Garrett was writing from a house located on Bowen's land. John Timberlake lived two miles west of Mirador. George Farrow lived three miles west of it.

240. Lyons, "Brooksville African-American Community, 1850–1880."

241. Freedmen's Bureau Online, familysearch.org. Data extracted by Sam Towler.

242. U.S. Pardons Under Amnesty Proclamations 1865–1869 for George Farrow, Ancestry.com; Death Indexing Project, online catalog, Images and Indexes, Library of Virginia.

243. A.P. Pianaway, "Sidetracking Crozet's Tunnel," *Richmond Times Dispatch*, November 30, 1941, 1; Hunter and Dooley, *Claudius Crozet*, 178; Couper, *Southern Sketches*, 181.

244. *Richmond Daily Dispatch*, December 12, 1862; Burke, *Mineral Springs*, 113–14; *Frank Leslie's Chimney Corner*, "Self-made Man," 214.

245. Turner, *Chessie's Road*, 50, 61–63.

246. Nelson, *Chesapeake and Ohio*, 63–64, 146; *Richmond Whig*, "The Covington Celebration," August 6, 1867, 4.

247. Turner, *Chessie's Road*, 72–73; *Alexandria Gazette*, February 27, 1872. Scott Reynolds Nelson maintains in *Steel Drivin' Man* that John Henry died at Lewis Tunnel in 1873 and that Claiborne Rice Mason, in effect, killed him.

248. Federal Census, Alleghany County, VA, 1870, shows that the widow and children of John Larguey, who died suddenly in July 1858, were living in Denis Shanahan's household with his immediate family; *Richmond Whig*, "Light Through Mud Tunnel," November 19, 1869, 3.

249. Nelson, *Chesapeake and Ohio*, 143.

250. Majewski, *A House Dividing*, 132.

251. Turner, *Chessie's Road*, 73, 92.

252. According to *Acts and Joint Resolutions Passed by the General Assembly of the State of Virginia During the Session of 1883–84*, Kelly sued the Board of Public Works in 1881 for money lost due to the repayment with bonds below par. He won, and the general assembly finally paid him $15,000, including interest, in 1884; *Frank Leslie's Chimney Corner*, 214.

253. Moorman, *Mineral Springs of North America*, 18; Coleman, "Virginia Central Railroad," 281–82; Silber, *Romance of Reunion*, 69–70.

254. Moorman, *Mineral Springs*, 61.

255. Allen Hale to the author, August 20, 2014; *New York Times*, "A Negro Murder[er] Hanged," November 6, 1880, 5; *Staunton Spectator*, September 10, 1910.

256. *North American and U.S. Gazette*, September 29, 1870; Lowell, MA *Daily Citizen*, November 26, 1877; *Washington Post*, "C&O Clears Tracks After Virginia Slide," October 22, 1942.

257. Logan, Barnard S., *Chesapeake and Ohio Historical Magazine* 30 (1998): 11.

258. *Richmond Times Dispatch*, "First Train Scheduled to Use C&O Tunnel on Thursday," March 26, 1944, 4-B; *Richmond Times Dispatch*, "Work Is Rapid on Afton Tunnel," July 7, 1942, 4; *Richmond Times Dispatch*, "Drilling on

Tunnel Is Completed," June 22, 1943, 8; *Railway Age*, "Eliminates Old Tunnels to Remove Restrictions to Traffic," January 8, 1944; *Richmond Times Dispatch*, "Questions and Answers," February 15, 1945, 13.

259. *Richmond Times Dispatch*, June 23, 1891.

260. Brackett descendant to the author, May 20, 2014; Blue Ridge Railroad contracts for slave labor, 1854, BRR; Federal Census, Albemarle County, VA, 1880. Dr. Charles C. Carter of Charlottesville, Virginia, leased the Brackett brothers' labor to the railroad. See *Blue Ridge Tunnel*, 174.

261. Hanley descendant to the author, May 7, 2014; Blue Ridge Tunnel payrolls, BRR.

262. Cecil Sharp, "Cecil Sharp's Appalachian Diaries, 1915–1918"; Vaughn Williams Memorial Library, http://www.vwml.org. Sharp collected some of the songs at Royal Orchards on Afton Mountain at Rockfish Gap, where Clinton and Florence lived in a rented farmhouse. When Karpeles returned in 1950, she recorded Florence in nearby Afton, Virginia.

263. Maud Karpeles, "Appalachian Diary," September 8, 1950–October 5, 1850, Vaughn Williams Memorial Library, http://www.vwml.org/record MK/6/1.

264. Ibid.; Sharp, "Appalachian Diaries"; Federal Census, Albemarle County, VA, 1870, 1880; Virginia Marriages, 1740–1850, Ancestry.com; Wallace store ledger, Greenwood, VA, 1852. Public records list Florence's mother with a different first name and the interchangeable McDaniel/McDonald surname: Berdie Lee McDaniel and Elizabeth McDonald. Florence told Cecil Sharp that her father was Irish; she likely meant that he was of Irish descent. It was her great-grandfather John McDaniel (also McDonald) who was born in Ireland.

265. Puckett, "Pat Do This," 1976.

Watchman at the Blue Ridge Tunnel

266. Gladys Wiltshire Burd, "History of the Scheeler Family," typescript, n.d., author's collection.

BIBLIOGRAPHY

Adams, Sean Patrick. *Dictionary of Virginia Biography*. Richmond: Library of Virginia, 2006.

Barton, William U. Account Book, 1851–1868. Private collection.

Board of Public Works. Papers, Railroads, Box 2, 1849–1851. Library of Virginia, Richmond, VA.

——. Papers, Railroads, Box 3, 1852–1858. Library of Virginia, Richmond, VA.

Burke, William. *Mineral Springs of Western Virginia; with Remarks on Their Use and the Diseases to Which They Are Applicable*. New York: Wiley and Putnam, 1842.

Coleman, Elizabeth Dabney. "The Story of the Virginia Central Railroad." PhD diss., University of Virginia, 1957.

Couper, Colonel William. *Southern Sketches Number 8 First Series Claudius Crozet Soldier-Scholar-Educator-Engineer*. Charlottesville, VA: Historical Publishing, 1936.

Derby, George, and James Terry White. *National Cyclopedia of American Biography*. Vol. 4. New York: J.T. White, 1904.

Dilts, James D. *The Great Road: The Building of the Baltimore and Ohio, the Nation's First Railroad, 1828–1853*. Stanford, CA: Stanford University Press, 1993.

Donnelly, James S. *Captain Rock: The Irish Agrarian Rebellion of 1821–1824*. Madison: University of Wisconsin Press, 2009.

Doyle, David Noel. "The Remaking of Irish America." In *Making the Irish American: History and Heritage of the Irish in the United States*, edited by J.J. Lee and Marion R. Casey. New York: New York University Press, 2006, 213–52.

Drinker, Henry Sturgis. *Tunneling, Explosives, and Rock Drills.* New York: John Wiley & Sons, 1882.

Duffy, Peter. *Killing of Major Denis Mahon: A Mystery of Old Ireland.* New York: Harper, 2007.

Dunn, Mary Lee. *Ballykilcline Rising: From Famine Ireland to Immigrant America.* Amherst: University of Massachusetts Press, 2008.

"Eliminates Old Tunnels to Remove Restrictions to Traffic." *Railway Age* 116 (1944): 143–46.

Ellet, Charles, Jr. *Mountain Top Track: A Description of the Railroad Across the Blue Ridge at Rockfish Gap in the State of Virginia.* Philadelphia: T.K. and P.G. Collins, 1856.

———."Railroad Across the Blue Ridge Mountains, Virginia, U.S." *Civil Engineer and Architect's Journal* 20 (1857): 190–91.

Ely, Melvin Patrick. *Israel on the Appomattox: A Southern Experiment in Black Freedom from the 1790s through the Civil War.* New York: Knopf, 2005.

Fogarty, Gerald P. *Commonwealth Catholicism: A History of the Catholic Church in Virginia.* Notre Dame, IN: University of Notre Dame Press, 2001.

Giemza, Bryan. "Turned Inside Out: Black, White, and Irish in the South." *Southern Cultures* 18 (2012): 34–57.

Gleeson, David. *Irish in the South, 1815–1877.* Chapel Hill: University of North Carolina Press, 2001.

Herrin, Dean. *America Transformed: Engineering and Technology in the Nineteenth Century: Selections from the Historic American Engineering Record.* National Park Service, Washington, D.C.: ASCE Press, 2002.

Hobbs, T. Gibson. *Canal on the James: An Illustrated Guide to James River Kanawha Canal.* Lynchburg, VA: Blackwell Press, 2009.

Holladay, Mary Jane Boggs. "Diary of Mary Jane Boggs Holladay 1851–1861." Charlottesville, [1970]. Albert and Shirley Small Special Collections, University of Virginia.

Hunter, Robert F., and Edwin L. Dooley. *Claudius Crozet: French Engineer in America, 1790–1864.* Charlottesville: University Press of Virginia, 1989.

Johnson, Aquila Peyton. "Diary of Aquila Johnson Peyton 1859–1861." Microfilm 646. Albert and Shirley Small Special Collections, University of Virginia.

Laxton, Edward. *Famine Ships: The Irish Exodus to America.* New York: Henry Holt & Co., 1996.

Lewis, Samuel. *Topographical Dictionary of Ireland.* London: S. Lewis and Company, 1837.

Logan, Barnard S. *Chesapeake and Ohio Historical Magazine* 30 (1998): 3–15.

Lyons, Mary E. *The Blue Ridge Tunnel: A Remarkable Engineering Feat in Antebellum Virginia*. Charleston, SC: The History Press, 2014.

Majewski, John. *A House Dividing: Economic Development in Pennsylvania and Virginia Before the Civil War*. Cambridge, UK: Cambridge University Press, 2000.

McIinnis, Maurie D. *Slaves Waiting for Sale: Abolitionist Art and the American Slave Trade*. Chicago: University of Chicago Press, 2013.

Middleton, William D. *Landmarks on the Iron Road: Two Centuries of North American Railroad Engineering*. Bloomington: Indiana University Press, 1998.

Moorman, John Jennings. *Mineral Springs of North America: How to Reach, and How to Use Them*. Philadelphia: J.B. Lippincott, 1873.

Morton, Oren F. *Annals of Bath County Virginia*. Staunton, VA: McClure Co., 1917.

Nelson, James Poyntz. *Chesapeake and Ohio Railway Company*. Richmond, VA: Lewis Printing Company, 1927.

Nelson, Scott Reynolds. *Steel Drivin' Man: John Henry, the Untold Story of an American Legend*. New York: Oxford University Press, 2006.

O'Brien, John. "Factory, Church, and Community: Blacks in Antebellum Richmond." *Journal of Southern History* 44 (1978): 509–36.

Perry, Jay Martin. "Shillelaghs, Shovels, and Secrets: Irish Immigrants and Secret Societies and the Building of Indiana Internal Improvements, 1835–1837." Master's thesis, Indiana University, 2009.

Peyton, J. Lewis. *History of Augusta County*. Staunton, VA: Yost & Son, 1882.

Puckett, Florence Fitzgerald. "Pat Do This, Pat Do That." *Cumberland Gap Maud Karpeles Collection*. Folktrax (CD 908), 1976.

Robertson, James I., Jr. *Stonewall Jackson: The Man, the Soldier, the Legend*. New York: Macmillan, 1997.

Scally, Robert James. *End of Hidden Ireland: Rebellion, Famine, & Emigration*. New York: Oxford University Press, 1995.

Scheele, Robert Blain. "'Oh Luce': A Young Lady Experiences the Union Army Invasion of Albemarle, March 1865." *Magazine of Albemarle County History* 61 (2003): 80–93.

"Self-made Man of Our Times, John Kelly." *Frank Leslie's Chimney Corner* 17 (1873): 214.

Silber, Nina. *Romance of Reunion: Northerners and the South, 1865–1890*. Chapel Hill: University of North Carolina Press, 1993.

Towler, Sam. *The Court Doth Order: Extracts from Albemarle County & Charlottesville, VA Order, Law Order, & Minute Books, 1800–1900*. Athens, GA: New Papyrus Publishing, 2008.

————. "New York, Albemarle and Surrounding Farms." Research project presented to Central Virginia History Researchers, Charlottesville, VA, 2014.

Trautwine, John C. *The Civil Engineer's Pocket Book*. Philadelphia: Trautwine, 1911.

Turner, Charles W. *Chessie's Road*. Richmond, VA: Garrett & Massie, 1956.

Virginia Central Railroad Company. Records, 1837–1869. Microform reels 4587–4590. Library of Virginia, Richmond, VA.

Waddell, Joseph. *Annals of Augusta County, Virginia*. Staunton, VA: Russell Caldwell, 1902.

Wallace, William. Wallace store ledger, 1851–1852. Greenwood, VA. Private collection.

Watson, J.C. *Chesapeake & Ohio Tunnels*. Clifton Forge, VA: Chesapeake & Ohio Historical Society, 2014.

Way, Peter. *Common Labour: Workers and the Digging of North American Canals, 1780–1860*. Cambridge, UK: Cambridge University Press, 1993.

Wooley, Carolyn Murray, and Karl Ratz. *Rock Fences of the Bluegrass: Architecture, Archaeology, and Landscape*. Lexington: University Press of Kentucky, 1992.

Index

ABOUT THE AUTHOR

Mary E. Lyons is the author of *The Blue Ridge Tunnel: A Remarkable Engineering Feat in Antebellum Virginia*, published by The History Press in 2014. She has also written nineteen books for young readers published by Scribner, Atheneum, Henry Holt, Houghton Mifflin and Oxford University Press. Born and raised in the American South, she holds dual Irish-U.S. citizenship, thanks to her Irish grandfather, Patrick Lyons. Born in 1869 in County Donegal, province of Ulster, he immigrated in 1884. He settled in Atlanta, Georgia, around 1900. Mary Lyons lives in Charlottesville, Virginia, with her husband, Paul.